FLYING HIGH

Also by S. Melvin Rines

The Supranationals
Al Gordon of Kidder Peabody

FLYING HIGH

The Story of a Fighter Pilot

S. MELVIN RINES

This book was printed in the United States of America.

To order additional copies of this book, contact:
Xlibris Corporation
1-888-795-4274
www.Xlibris.com
Orders@Xlibris.com
28739

To my grandchildren and their's . . . .

This is the way it was.

CONTENTS

Part 4
Marriage and a New Career

ACKNOWLEDGMENTS

To my wife Mary Jo, I am grateful for her support, creative suggestions, and forbearance during the writing of this book. And to my children, Marcy and David, my heartfelt thanks for their reactions and comments on the story, and frequent technical advice when my computer misbehaved. My brother, Stan, sister-in-law, Nina, and niece, Carole Ziter, contributed and corroborated content and detail on the early chapters for which I am grateful.

I thank Louie Holland for encouraging me to turn what began as a personal account for my grandchildren into a book. A professional in the publishing field, his inspiration and knowledge of the arcane art of writing-for-publication was crucial. I am especially grateful for the friendship and able assistance of John Rousmaniere, acclaimed author of many books, for taking time to comment and add structure to the story. And my thanks to Maureen Baron, a professional editor, for the vital cutting and arranging so necessary to make a workable manuscript readable.

The book has benefited from Tilbury House publisher, Jennifer Bunting's critical suggestions, and the thoughtful comments of my friends Mary Avery and Titia Bozuwa, the latter a successful author in her own right. And, lastly, my thanks to "Whitey" Lichtfuss and other members of VF-721, for their remembrances and photographs,

Despite all this help, responsibility for content is mine alone. Every effort has been made to provide an accurate account of the events depicted but I am mindful that, like all memoirs, much depends on the individual writer's impressions and memories of those events, most of which go back more than half a century.

PROLOGUE

Y ou lived and died alone, especially in fighters. Fighters. Somehow, despite everything, that word had not become sterile. You slipped into the hollow cockpit and strapped and plugged yourself into the machine. The canopy ground shut and sealed you off. Your oxygen, your very breath, you carried with you into the chilled vacuum, in a steel bottle. If you wanted to speak, you used the radio. You were as isolated as a deep sea diver, only you went up, into nothing, instead of down.

—James Salter
Gods of Tin
The Flying Years
Shoemaker and Hoad
Washington DC 2004

Growing up in the Great Depression, coming of age in World War II, my passion was to fly—my dream to be a fighter pilot. This is the story of how that passion and dream converged into reality and fifty-five combat missions over Korea.

—S. Melvin Rines
October 2005

Part 1

THE FORMATIVE YEARS

*F*ollowing the 1929 stock market crash, a worldwide Depression washed over the nation, destroying savings, jobs, and eventually, hope as it deepened and spread through the 1930s. No area in the country was immune, certainly not my hometown in New Hampshire where one of two major companies collapsed and the other limped on in an ever-descending spiral of crises and failed initiatives. Despite an avalanche of job-creating programs to stimulate the economy, it took the war in Europe and the inevitable involvement of America before the country's industrial power revived and people went back to work.

It was during this period—one like few others in history—that my passion to become a fighter pilot was kindled and much of the educational and psychological development so peculiar to making one took place. When the Japanese attacked Pearl Harbor in 1941, plunging the nation into war, the opportunity to enlist in military flight training surfaced; and I was ready.

CHAPTER 1

GROWING UP IN A MILL TOWN

The hand-painted sign read Airport—with an arrow pointing down a winding dirt road. It led past a corrugated metal hangar with a high roof and wall-sized door—home to three airplanes and a collection of used parts, tools, and half-filled paint cans. Huddled beside the hangar was a small building with peeling white paint and unwashed windows, serving at once as office, lounge, and locker room for the handful of flyers using the field. Just outside a front door that never quite closed was a long wooden bench nestled in the tall grass, the sole concession to the occasional visitor.

Parked haphazardly in front of the hangar were a Piper Cub, a Curtis biplane, and a low-wing monoplane of uncertain heritage, waiting quietly—almost forlornly—to take to the air. The airfield itself was a little more than a grass strip undulating through a pasture, with a windsock snapping in the breeze. A soft silence pervaded the area, almost begging to be broken as the early morning sun peeked through. It was hardly a scene to stir one's soul—unless you were a twelve-year-old boy and your head swirled with dreams of flying.

I had left home at eight that morning and pedaled more than four miles to hang around, eavesdrop on pilots, gaze worshipfully at airplanes, and hope to see one take off. The year was 1936, and the miracle of flight was upon us. The glow from Lindbergh's flight across the Atlantic was less than a decade old,

3

and other records were being set almost daily. Yet no one I knew had ever been up in an airplane, and most of us still ran outside to watch and marvel when one flew over. Happiness for me was sitting on that long bench, listening to laconic tales of flight from a small band of aviators, and wishing I were one of them.

Johnny West, a pilot straight out of Central Casting, managed the airport and was one of the fortunate few able to make a living in aviation. He not only flew planes, he also kept them flying, as a master mechanic and all-round troubleshooter. Handsome, slender, his black hair combed flat, and a thin mustache gracing his upper lip, he lived the part of a glamorous airman, transporting passengers and priority packages over the North Country, and— his bread and butter—taking people up for brief sightseeing rides. I loved to watch him in worn leather jacket and sunglasses, stride toward his bright yellow Piper Cub with a nervous passenger (who had paid in advance) in tow.

West briefed the passenger on what to expect and the sights to look for, while strapping him into the front seat. Then, after a quick walk-around inspection of the plane, he settled in the backseat, checked his instruments, and began a crisp exchange of commands. It was "Switch off," "Switch on," and "Contact"— each repeated, in sequence, by a fellow pilot or trusted hanger-on waiting to spin the propeller. And then—and only then—the prop was spun vigorously and repeatedly until the engine coughed into life. I watch transfixed as he taxied out, took off, and disappeared over the horizon.

Occasionally, West went up alone to deliver a package or perhaps sell rides at another airport, and I'd arrange to be in his path as he headed out to the plane. My abiding fantasy, one that kept me coming back, was that one day he would stop, casually look around, and say, "Hey, kid, what d'ya say? Would you like to go up for a spin?" Then I would be in the front seat, soaring into a cloudless sky to the mysterious world beyond.

But, alas, it never happened. He rarely noticed me and never spoke as he hurried on his way. Yet, through a faint imaginary scrim of the future, I could see shimmering images of other flights in more powerful planes, going well beyond those childhood dreams. And it was I in the leather jacket and sunglasses, and I was at the controls.

Transformed and enlarged by time and circumstance, many of those images blossomed into life—some, at this very airport.

In 1924, the year I was born, Berlin, New Hampshire, was known as the paper-manufacturing center of the world. Nestled in the foothills of the White Mountains, just seventy miles south of the Canadian border, more than twenty thousand inhabitants lived and worked along a winding, almost-picturesque river. Dominating the center of town and running parallel to its main street was a sprawling mill quietly emitting streams of thin white smoke slowly drifting over the surrounding forests. Then and now, from a distance, Berlin appeared idyllic—a typical New England mill town. But a closer view revealed a river less inviting, a mill more oppressive, and a distinctly unpleasant odor emanating from that smoke. It was anything but idyllic.

Two flourishing enterprises, Brown Company and the International Paper Company, each noted for its pioneering and manufacturing efficiencies, had made Berlin the leading producer of newsprint and paper products in the country. Their payrolls and the businesses that grew up around them provided the financial underpinning for Berlin's citizens, and the mills' around-the-clock, seven-day-week work schedules were the pulse and heartbeat of the town's life. Making paper required long hours and hard work but few skills, so the mills attracted newly arrived immigrants, many from Europe and the Middle East, but most from nearby French-speaking Canada, all seeking a foothold in their new country. As these immigrants streamed in, they settled in ethnic enclaves, established their own churches and schools, and gradually, over time, melted into larger, distinct neighborhoods.

Paper manufacturing is a continuous process of cutting, transporting, and chipping trees to be cooked ("digested") in a mixture of chemicals. The resulting slurry is pressed into pulp, to be converted then or later into a variety of products and grades of paper. The process was a marvel to see, and the end product vital to everyday life. But sadly, it came with a price: a highly toxic, foul-smelling steam that was frequently vented into the air and left to waft over town by whatever winds and downdrafts existed at the moment. At times, it would quite literally take one's breath away.

If that weren't bad enough, the spent mixture of chemicals and wood pitch was routinely discharged into the Androscoggin River, turning its water a frothy orange, uninhabitable for any living organism. There were few environmental regulations at the time and no public outcry against this noxious assault on the quality of life. The consciousness of company officials, the public, and indeed, the entire country, had simply not reached that level. When asked why he didn't complain, a townsman would simply shrug his shoulders, and say, "That's just the way it is."

Yet despite the gray presence of the mills and their impact on our lives, Berlin was a wonderful place to grow up in. There were lakes to swim in, brooks for fishing, and mountains to climb, and in the winter, vast expanses for sledding, skating, and skiing. The small-town atmosphere, relative isolation, and common employment fostered close relationships, bridging economic and cultural divides; and the mingling of Yankee mores with old-world conventions softened ethnic and social distinctions. Out of this cultural mix, supported by a loving family, taught by dedicated teachers, and blessed with good fortune, I somehow managed to see over the horizon, define success, and revel in its pursuit. I wouldn't change a thing.

My parents, Gladys Olive Estes and William James Rines, were barely in their twenties when they arrived in Bretton Woods, New Hampshire, in 1912. This resort town was the home of the grand old Mount Washington Hotel, still standing and famous for the Bretton Woods Agreement that created a new international monetary system, the World Bank and IMF, in 1944. It was where the elite, with their steamer trunks, flocked in June to relax and play for the summer.

My father drove a team of horses and a carriage to pick up passengers at the local train station and take them and their trunks to the hotel some three miles away. One of those passengers (but with no trunk) was a striking young woman with reddish hair from Brewer, Maine, who had arrived to wait on tables. Intrigued, William made an uncommon effort to make her feel comfortable in her new surroundings, and Gladys was quick to show her appreciation. She had never been away from Maine and the farm where she was born, or the school she had left at the eighth grade to "help with the chores."

My father had also dropped out of school to work on his family's farm, and at fourteen, drive a team of horses hauling lumber out of the woods during the winter in nearby Cherry Mountain. Both families were early arrivals from England (my father's reputedly in 1634), and neither branch had strayed far from its original homestead in the intervening years. My parents were highly intelligent, though unschooled; hardworking, but not driven; and eminently comfortable with their lives and fortune.

The courtship began the moment Gladys smiled at him. William took pains to impress her with his horsemanship and was especially helpful with her luggage. She was suitably awed by his skill and managed to need more help than would seem necessary for a farm girl. Later on, they kept bumping into each other during and after work. Casual conversation blossomed into friendship. They toiled long hours, seven days a week, in and around the huge resort hotel, but still found time to hike in the surrounding mountains, enjoy the camaraderie of other young workers, and discover a miraculous similarity in their interests. They were married in the fall.

Shortly thereafter, they migrated some thirty miles north to Berlin where my father joined an older brother in the railroad division of the Brown Company. I remember my father being tall, strong, soft spoken, and even-tempered; while my mother, of medium height and build, was vocal and determined, holding and readily sharing strong opinions on almost any subject. She seemed to have free rein on most family matters as long as his assumed authority as head of household was honored. If threatened, however, that authority was asserted quietly but firmly; and everyone understood that it was not subject to debate. They showed great affection for each other, openly displayed, radiating emotional warmth throughout the family.

I was the youngest of four children. My sister Geraldine was the first born, followed by Lloyd, Stanley, and me at three-year intervals. We lived on the upper two floors of a two-family house my parents purchased in the early-1920s. The first floor was rented to the same family for over twenty years, making them almost an extension of our own. Their weekly rent money was paid in cash, always on time, and immediately deposited in a sugar bowl in a kitchen cabinet. That bowl also received part of my father's weekly paycheck, along with any other money saved during the month. On the day interest on the house mortgage was due, my father would empty the bowl, walk to the bank, and pay the interest owed, and although not required, apply the remainder to reduce principal. It was the only debt my parents had, and they couldn't wait to get rid of it.

The lower of our two upper floors consisted of a kitchen, dining room, an infrequently used "parlor," bedrooms for my parents and Gerry, and one bathroom. On the upper floor, Lloyd had his own bedroom, and Stan and I shared the other larger one. How all managed to use that one bathroom equitably, especially on Saturday nights, is fortunately lost in memory—although I recall sibling impatience with our teenage sister "just in there primping." Stan and I, closest in age, engaged in the usual arguments and pillow fights, swapped all childhood diseases, and shared plans and dreams for the future before going to sleep.

Many of those dreams were sparked by a nearby Boston and Maine train whistle that pierced the night on schedule, calling up places not seen, challenges unmet, and unimaginable wonders to come. One particularly exciting and recurring dream sequence revolved around flying, prompted by the exploits of "G-8 and His Battle Aces" serialized in a popular pulp magazine. These three World War I fighter pilots in their double-winged Spads always managed to defeat the Boche in their Fokkers in swirling battles in the air, and even a few on the ground after being shot down. The writing was lurid and heroics grand, and I counted the days until the next adventure arrived at our neighborhood drugstore.

Stan and I reenacted many of those dogfights by creating virtual Spads on our back porch. We placed two chairs side by side and built makeshift wooden frames around them. Then, with sawed-off broom handles for joysticks and cardboard dials tacked on a half-moon block of wood for instruments, we covered them with blankets. When the attack sirens sounded, we "climbed" into our respective cockpits, pulled the blankets over our heads, revved up, took off, and swooped in on the enemy. With machine guns *rat-a tat-tatting* amid excited shouts of incoming aircraft and flak, we took on all comers, usually against great odds. We always emerged victorious.

My formative years were spent in a busy, largely cooperative household where each of us was assigned at least one daily chore, which we reflexively pronounced unfair compared to the other assignments. As the youngest, my servitude progressed over the years from setting the table to drying dishes, and when strong enough, keeping the furnace and kitchen stove supplied. With no central heating, we relied on an all-purpose wood-and-coal stove in the kitchen for cooking and hot water and a coal-burning furnace radiating almost enough heat to be comfortable for the rest of the house.

In the winter, my father banked the fires each night before retiring and rekindled them at 5:30 the following morning. My mother rose around 6:00 to oversee a breakfast melee of four children busily pouring cereal, cooking eggs, and making toast. Then, before sending us off to school, she lined us up, with a bottle of cod liver oil in one hand and a teaspoon in the other, which she filled to overflowing, and administered between gulps of orange juice. "It will ward off colds," she assured us—and I became a lifelong believer.

If breakfasts were chaotic, "dinners" (at noon) and suppers were relatively sedate family affairs. We each had an assigned place at the table, carefully selected to minimize sibling poking, bumping, arguing, or complaining. My father presumably reigned over the proceedings, but my mother ruled. Ad hoc discussions of the day's activities unfolded, punctuated by frequent admonitions to eat more, eat less, sit still, or be quiet. The menu was hearty, healthy, and predictable, especially the ubiquitous New England boiled dinner, and of course, the obligatory baked beans on Saturday night. Permission to leave the table was required.

We were a happy family, genuinely fond and protective of each other, and armed with a clear understanding of the differences between right and wrong as defined by our parents. These were not hazy concepts, but rather dictums from on high, allowing little equivocation and no appeals. When violated, disciplinary action was swift and sure, and almost always meted out by my mother. My father, on the other hand, obtained much the same result merely by threat or menacing look. These contrasting styles and their perceived relative success caused tension between them and amusement among us. My mother's prima facie evidence that her method was superior was the story (often recounted within earshot of my father) that she overheard one of us say, "When Dad catches us doing something wrong, he just scolds us and warns the next time we will be punished. But when Mom catches us, we *know* we will get a licking."

In reality, those "lickings" were few and far between, mostly due to her methodical prestrike planning. She kept her prime weapon—a whip—handy and in plain view in the kitchen. Whenever arguments or skirmishes got out of hand, she had only to reach for it to secure the battleground. It always worked because we knew the threat was real. I recall one time Lloyd told her he was going to visit someone for the evening, and instead went somewhere else, which was forbidden. When she happened to find out, we were all informed of the transgression. Lying was serious business, so we knew he was "in for it." We stayed awake until he came home and then eavesdropped as she loudly stated the facts of the case, the gravity of the offense, and the punishment required. The dreaded whip went to work. The yelps commenced, crescendoed, and then subsided into sobs as he was sent to bed. The next morning, Lloyd was chastened but unmarked, and the rest of us behaved uncommonly well.

My father and mother were "good Baptists," and we kids all fought and lost the argument against attending Sunday school. The religious disciplines of the day were quite severe. Central to Baptist doctrine was the non-negotiable "no work and no play on Sundays" rule. That meant no card playing or movies and no cowboy games or "racing around the house."

Alcohol of any kind was forbidden; and of course, neither of them ever drank, though my father kept a pint of whiskey in a kitchen cabinet for those rare occasions when a bad cold required "hot toddy" for survival—under the watchful eye of my mother, of course. Still, he frequently went on hunting and fishing trips with his more freewheeling brothers, and who knew what heinous concoctions were consumed. Our mother's view of demon rum was simple and pure and was summarized in her oft-spoken declaration that "If liquor never touches your lips, you will never crave it."

Fortunately, as we grew older, they were able to adjust to the changing mores and attitudes (but never to jitterbugging) of the new generation. They eventually relaxed many of the strictures, confident they had armed us with the tenets of good behavior and high moral standards, and left it to us to abide by them—a priceless legacy.

Our backyard was an integral part of our circumscribed universe; and although quite small, it seemed vast to our young eyes. It was lined with a woodshed and henhouse on one side, a garage on the other, and the back of a neighbor's barn at the end. The yard became a kaleidoscope of highly constricted, always-contentious games of baseball, football, croquet, hopscotch, boxing, and whatever else we could think of.

At times, various structures would sprout up that we built from old boards and straightened nails scavenged from around the neighborhood. Especially vexing to my parents was a camp that started out on stilts and that could only be accessed by ladder through a trapdoor. Stan and his friends built it, ostensibly to ensure privacy—no doubt to exclude me and my friends. When none of us seemed to care, they enclosed the stilts, making additional camp space available. I remember my father shaking his head and saying, "It's the first time I ever saw the upper floor of a two-story house built first."

Another time, Stan and a friend were building a "house" high in our tall backyard tree when a supporting limb broke. I arrived shortly after they hit the ground, to see my mother washing Stan's face and consoling him. He was crying and gasping for breath, having had the wind knocked out of him. His friend was being tended for what turned out to be a badly broken leg, sadly, one that left him with a pronounced limp for the rest of his life.

My father handled most of the backyard chaos with relative equanimity—until the day we chose up sides and recreated World War I. We had dug opposing trenches with various obstructions between them and were busily firing our guns (sticks) and throwing grenades (mud balls) when he arrived home from work. He ordered an immediate ceasefire, dressed us down, and started in on the area commander, my mother. He was just getting up to pitch when she interrupted with, "I'd rather have them playing here where I can keep an eye on them instead of worrying about what they were doing somewhere else." The commander carried the day.

I do not recall an acrimonious argument or overt display of anger between my mother and father. Major disagreements were either resolved when we weren't around or were dealt with by her celebrated "silent treatment." This unannounced and unexplained tactic only became apparent when she simply stopped talking to him—about anything. The reason for invoking the treatment was seldom clear to us and possibly to my father. However, he would take it in stride without comment or complaint, apparently confident that it would be transitory.

In the meantime, we kids served as interlocutors. It went something like this: "Dad, Mom wants to know if you will stop at the store on your way to work." Dad: "Tell your mother I can't or I will be late." Mom: "Then ask your father why he can't leave a little earlier." "Dad, Mom wants to know why you can't leave a little earlier." Or when my father failed to get a direct response from her, he might say, "Stanley, ask your mother if she will iron my shirts for tomorrow." "Mom, Dad wants to know if you will iron his shirts for tomorrow." Mom: "Tell your father he will just have to wait and see." And so on. We would convey each message, replicating tone and inflection precisely, and most of the time the ice would just melt away. In any event, the silent treatment seldom carried into the next day—they slept in a double bed.

Our medical needs, and they were considerable over the years, were handled by our family doctor. He was always referred to as "Doc" Pulsifer; I never knew his first name. He was heavyset, always wore a suit and a vest (with pocket watch and chain), and was rumpled, kindly, and unhurried—right out of a Norman Rockwell painting. He had delivered all four children (in our home); nursed us through all the childhood diseases, including scarlet fever, diphtheria, and rheumatic fever; and set broken bones; bandaged wounds; and removed tonsils, appendixes, and occasionally, teeth. House calls were the norm. I remember only one visit to his office, a study in chaos. Heavy, worn furniture sat on ancient carpets, and papers and boxes were scattered everywhere, especially boxes. They had to be removed from the scale before weighing, from his desk before writing, and would have had to be removed from the floor if vacuumed. Yet he seemed oblivious to it all and always knew exactly where to find anything he needed.

We had complete faith in him. I can still hear my father say, "Old Doc Pulsifer doesn't need to examine patients; he can tell what's wrong just by looking at you." And we all believed it. One day, when I was very young, I remember seeing chairs being removed from around the kitchen table, a blanket covered by a white bed sheet spread on the table, and kettles of water boiling on the stove. Doc Pulsifer was dressed as usual, except he had taken off his suit coat and rolled up his sleeves. Then I was ushered into another room, told to be quiet, and the door was closed.

I learned later that Lloyd was having his tonsils removed; and while he was still under ether, Pulsifer decided to pull an aching tooth as well. The combination apparently caused excessive bleeding, and Lloyd stopped breathing. Pulsifer quickly resuscitated him by emergency measures never explained to me. Such was his standing that he was praised for "saving Lloyd's life," and the wisdom of combining the two surgical procedures went unquestioned. He was, after all, like a member of the family, taking care of us diligently and sympathetically for as long as we could remember—truly dedicated and compassionate, doing his best with the medical knowledge available.

The Great Depression was in full swing, money was tight, and everyone was economizing. Many consumers were buying "on time," but our family never did. Cars, furniture, even major house repairs were paid for in cash saved in advance. My father's steady job and his conservative money management enabled us to survive the Depression without true hardship. We always had an automobile, for example, and adequate food and clothing. Most of my friends were not as fortunate. I remember playing after school with friends in their threadbare "rents," where out-of-work fathers lolled around while mothers worked and worried, looking shopworn and wan. And I remember walking with another friend along the railroad tracks, with a bucket, picking up stray pieces of coal for him to take home to burn. One friend's father paid us five cents for each empty liquor bottle we found—he never told us what he used them for; he didn't need to in those difficult prohibition times.

My mother bought food and vegetables when seasonally cheap to store or preserve, routinely baked bread and pastries, and sewed and mended when she had a moment to rest. There were no weekly allowances for children, so we worked at whatever odd jobs could be found. Mine included a newspaper route (for a penny a paper), setting up bowling pins (for three cents a string), and sawing firewood with a pal and two-handed "cross cut" saw (for a dollar a cord, split between us). I even borrowed a kit and shined shoes to finance a movie or milkshake when the need was sufficiently dire. Out of this experience emerged a lifelong proclivity to work and save that has served me well.

The first car I remember was a mid-1920s Dodge sedan, with wide running boards, isinglass windows, and a balky engine that required strenuous cranking by hand to start. Every outing was preceded by the caveat, "If the car starts," and the estimated time of arrival was predicated on "not getting a flat tire." The "windows" were rolled up and kept in the trunk, ready to be retrieved and snapped into place if rain or blustery weather threatened. One of the surest signs of an impending storm was to see a line of cars parked along a roadside, with drivers hastily snapping them on.

A brand-new 1930 Chrysler is the car I remember most clearly. To us it was the height of luxury, with its upholstered seats, real glass windows, and miracle of miracles, an electrically starting engine. And it had a top speed, reluctantly reached, of forty miles per hour! My father washed and polished it almost every

Sunday before church; and after a midday dinner, we would all pile in for a drive in the country. It didn't much matter where.

Most hills in the region required downshifting to surmount unless approached at high speed. At least once a month, my father would route us over Gorham Hill in a nearby town that was particularly challenging. To the dismay of my mother, he would turn into Barney Oldfield, that famous old-time race-car driver, as he approached the hill, careening around curves at top speed, to climb as high as the car would go before stalling. As it gradually lost speed, he would nurse the engine onward, and we would add body movement and cheers of encouragement. Then, when the inevitable happened and he was forced to downshift, we would take note of a rock or tree to mark the spot, and tuck it away into our collective memories as a goal to surpass the next time.

Challenges such as this, plus occasional diversionary stops for candy or ice cream, were entertainment enough to keep us coming back for more. It didn't matter how long we were underway or how badly we four kids behaved in the backseat, my parents always seemed to enjoy the drive. Perhaps it was simply a temporary escape from the worsening economic situation in Berlin.

Shortly after the Great Depression began in 1929, the International Paper Company closed down, leaving only the Brown Company to support the economic life of the community. In the best of times, paper manufacturing was a complex, capital-intensive process dependent on business and manufacturing cycles over which workers (and managers) had no control. In depressed periods, workers were "called in" only as needed, sometimes for as little as half a day; and there were no paid holidays or vacations and none of the health and unemployment benefits so common today. But it was the only game in town; and it kept food on the table, so everyone "made do."

My father was in charge of maintaining Brown Company's railroad operations. He made sure the company's steam engines and hundreds of owned and transient boxcars were kept in working condition, and that the tracks on which they ran were in good repair. He operated out of his own building, with a large machine shop and a crew of carpenters, machinists, and a blacksmith who collectively could repair, rebuild, or replace whatever rolled on the company's tracks.

When I was still a youngster, my father occasionally took me with him to see some of the major repair jobs underway and the machines used to do them. It was all very impressive to a little fellow, but what I remember most was the happy role of being the boss's son and basking in the overt friendliness of my dad's workers. He must have been a good manager, for I recall a clean, orderly work area, and ostensibly happy employees going about the messy business of sawing, bolting, welding, and hammering necessary to keep the equipment rolling. Although he no longer got his hands dirty, he seemed able to do any job in the department and enjoyed passing that knowledge on to his men.

His was an 8:00-to-5:00 job, with an hour off for "dinner" unless an accident or derailment occurred, and then it was work around the clock until the problem was solved. He always walked the two miles back and forth to work each day, regardless of weather, for the noon meal with his family. The fathers of most of my friends worked at jobs in the continuous paper-making process and were not as fortunate. They had to work rotating eight-hour shifts with only a thirty-minute lunchbox break, disrupting family routines, and complicating whatever social life they had. The worst shift, of course, was the twelve to eight, for it meant trying to keep kids quiet during the day so that father could sleep—a never-ending effort that was seldom successful.

Each worker rotated to the next shift weekly, "punching" in and out daily to get credit for time worked. Pay started around twenty-five cents per hour and was placed in cash in an envelope on Thursday, an important day in the life of the town. Bills were paid, purchases were made, and savings (if any) were set aside. "Beer joints" throughout the city were filled with workers celebrating their survival for one more week, while their wives waited anxiously for their family's "food money" to arrive. At the time, I was only vaguely aware of how bleak their lives were, especially during the long, bitter cold winters. They had few opportunities for advancement or increased pay, leaving most of them destined to spend their entire lives working at the same job.

At eight o'clock, after my father left for work and the kids were all off to school, my mother's work really began. Monday was wash day, with its unchanging routine of gathering dirty clothes, heating kettles of water, filling tubs, wringing, rinsing, wringing again, and finally hanging clothes out to dry. Almost everything was done by hand except for a motorized agitator that cranked away in a gray cast-iron Maytag washing machine. This marvel, kept in a corner of the kitchen and wheeled to the middle of the room (which, as a tot, I was allowed to ride), was perhaps the only improvement in washing clothes since the advent of running water. The entire operation took most of the day to accomplish.

Tuesday, set aside for baking, started by assembling numerous pots and pans, preparing various fillers and condiments, and stoking the fire to heat the oven. By nightfall there would be a fresh supply of pies, cookies, cakes, and doughnuts, surrounded by fresh loaves of bread for the week ahead. "Store bought" products were seldom seen (or missed) in our house, and home-baked bread remained the rule until the miraculous invention of sliced bread, an event so earthshaking I can remember exactly where I was when told about it. The rest of her week was devoted to cleaning, ironing, shopping, and being there when we came home from school. We never had a latchkey.

CHAPTER 2

SCHOOL DAYS

My formal education didn't begin until I entered first grade at King School on the east side of town since kindergartens were nonexistent, and nursery schools unknown. There were no buses or luncheon facilities, so I walked to school and back, twice a day, regardless of weather. Winters were particularly daunting. I was bundled in layers of clothing, heavy boots, a hat pulled over my ears, and a scarf wound around my face, making it difficult to walk, talk, and sometimes, see. Long underwear (the famous "union suits") were worn from the end of November to the first of April, and on wintry washdays, could be seen dancing stiffly in the wind on clotheslines all over town.

The school offered six grades with roughly twenty-five students in each, taught by strict, well-organized teachers. All female and single (married women were not employed in public schools), they taught reading, writing, and arithmetic, mostly by rote, to students with a wide range of capabilities but limited goals. Few sought more than passing grades, and most planned to quit school as soon as the law permitted. It was not, to say the least, a fertile place for aspiring young minds.

Remarkably, the teachers managed to educate those few who wanted to learn, and maintain discipline among the rest. Misbehaving students were kept after school, or if transgressions were serious enough, punished by the infamous *rubber hose.* Sentencing was swift and irreversible, and handed down with the dreaded order to "Go to the principal's office." There you would sit, often alone, and always incommunicado, until Ms. Flynn, the fiery redheaded principal, arrived. She would listen to the student's version of the crime, and compare it with the teacher's report, while coldly fingering a two-foot length of garden hose prominently displayed on her desk. Guilt was assumed, only the degree was at issue in determining the number of whacks applied, and whether on one hand or two.

By fourth grade, I had survived the rubber hose twice, hadn't cried, and was rising in stature when disaster struck. The *S* in S. Melvin stands for Sherley, an ordinary enough name, until Shirley Temple (female) became a child movie star, instantly branding me with a *girl's name.* I desperately pointed out to all who would listen that my first name was spelled with an *E* instead of an *I,* and that, as my parents constantly assured me, it was a boy's name. No matter, the taunting began and increased geometrically as the actress's popularity grew. I remember all too painfully being surrounded by kids chanting, "SHIRLEY TEMPLE, SHIRLEY TEMPLE, SHIRLEY TEMPLE," despite my futile efforts to silence them. Fortunately, "Chobe," a nickname of obscure origin, came to the rescue, and gradually ended the torment. As a young adult, I switched to my first initial and middle name, obscuring it from all but the most curious for years.

One of the immutable rites of passage for boys, especially at King School, was the need to fight. The bouts were episodic but frequent, and never very serious—just ordinary fistfights that often degenerated into wrestling matches with no clear winner. Any excuse—a misunderstood word, a shove, or a reputed insult—was enough to start one. To stand up and fight was vital to one's self-esteem regardless of outcome, and the status gained from actually winning was well worth an occasional bloody nose or black eye. I had my share of them (some due to that child actress with a *boy's* name), and I won enough to gain respect and keep the bullies at bay.

Perhaps the most memorable fight was the one that never happened. My erstwhile friend Chester Olmstead and I had an altercation during school recess;

tempers flared, and we were exchanging blows when the bell rang to return to class. Terribly angry, we vowed to meet for a fight to the finish in his backyard after school. Word of the impending battle spread like wildfire, and a crowd of kids gathered at the appointed time and place to watch the carnage. By then, of course, Chester and I were friends again, having forgotten why we were angry— if we ever really knew. But we couldn't disappoint the crowd, so we squared off, and feigning great fury, started swinging. After a number of relatively harmless body blows and assorted grunts and groans, the crowd seemed satisfied, so we quit, shook hands, and went off to play.

Although my grades were good, I didn't think of myself as smarter than my classmates. One day, while a group of us were hanging around, an argument broke out over the answer to an obscure question, and someone piped up with, "Ask Chobe, he'll know." I was surprised to be considered the local oracle, and pleased that I knew the answer. It was an epiphany of sorts for it prompted me to look at my standing in the class more critically, and for the first time, think beyond quitting school early to take a job. It proved life changing: I can think of only two others in that class who graduated from high school—and neither of them went on to college.

That summer, my mother heard that Ms. Haweeli, scheduled to be my sixth-grade teacher, was being transferred to another school about two miles across town. My mother knew her personally and felt strongly that I should be in her class, and somehow managed to get me transferred—no small feat in any bureaucratic system, and almost unheard of in Berlin. I must have sensed its importance for I willingly left my classmates, walked those extra miles daily, and quickly became immersed in an entirely new learning environment.

The new school served a slightly more upscale neighborhood with a different ethnic mix. Its academic goals were far more ambitious, and to my surprise, most classmates planned to finish high school, and some even talked of going on to college! Ms. Haweeli taught with such enthusiasm that students inevitably got caught up in the excitement of learning. I was surprised at how extensive homework assignments were, and that they had to be completed. After-school help was available, encouraged, and even used. Tests were carefully corrected, with many comments, and grades were important and had to be earned. She also went well beyond the required curriculum to discuss current events, local issues, and social etiquette.

For the latter, she engaged us in role-playing to make introductions, respond to greetings, and react to various social situations. Her quizzes and assignments included writing thank-you notes and responses to invitations, and even arranging silverware for a formal dinner. Perhaps most important, she insisted on "good manners" in everything we did. As a result, discipline was seldom a problem; we were kept too busy to act up. Julia Haweeli never married and had no children of her own, yet she undoubtedly shaped the destiny of hundreds of other children and their progeny. Hers was truly a noble career.

Summer vacations were wonderfully long, or so it seemed, and there were so many things to do like swimming, bike riding, hiking, and climbing mountains. And, of course, sandlot baseball was in its heyday; a time when kids just showed up at a local field, glove in hand, and if they wanted to be sure to be included, a ball or bat.

Two self-appointed "captains" would choose up sides, taking turns picking their teammates from those waiting to play. Field positions and batting orders evolved through contentious consensus; bases were fashioned out of stones, sand bags, or just lines in the dirt. There were no umpires, coaches, or fancy uniforms, and *no adults*—just kids making their own rules, and learning to abide by them. Games ended by agreement (or disagreement), or when the owner of the ball or bat went home. It was great fun.

When I was eight, my parents bought a large tent to take us camping on the Maine shore on holidays, and the following year, to Dolly Copp Campground in the heart of the White Mountain National Forest for the summer. My mother camped with all four children the first two weeks to make sure we could take care of ourselves, and then let my brothers and me camp on our own—my sister had decided she preferred boys to rustic living. We swam and fished in mountain streams, hiked all over the Presidential Range, and played the usual games with children of other campers, many of whom were teachers from out of state.

We built wood fires for cooking, a rock enclosure in a mountain stream for refrigeration, and lived well on basic foods and canned vegetables. When it rained, we subsisted on peanut butter and jelly sandwiches, and read books. I remember lying on my bunk for hours, listening to rain pelting the canvas roof, enthralled by the daring-do of cowboys, spies, and those World War I fighter pilots serialized in pulp magazines. Occasionally, even a book from our school's summer reading list would surface if it rained long enough.

My parents visited at least twice a week to replenish supplies and see that we were all right. They left reassured, and armed with a new shopping list for the next visit. Years later, when asked how three brothers could get along on their own, I responded only half in jest, "It was just a matter of command and control. You see, Lloyd might decide we needed more firewood, and tell Stan, who would determine what kind and how much—and then I would be sent out to get it." In truth, they always seemed to look after their younger brother, and I don't remember any serious fights or major disagreements. In subsequent years, when first Lloyd and then Stan went off to summer jobs, I invited various friends to join me. It all added up to marvelous summers for me and well-earned respites for my parents—and a sense of independence and self-reliance that helped prepare me for later military service.

Being the youngest brother had other advantages. One was the time-honored opportunity to extort money by being a pest, especially when young men came calling on my sister. Like others before me, I made the amazing discovery that if I hung around long enough, her dates (and sometimes even my sister) would slip me a nickel to disappear. One of her more ardent beaus brought along a guitar to croon to her in the parlor. I found this so interesting that I invited a friend to hide under the couch with me to listen to the singing and whatever else might transpire. When discovered, my sister was not amused.

Later, when Lloyd inexplicably began dating girls, I noticed they usually became more interested in me. I basked in their attention and occasional gifts of candy, and soon learned I could tell how much they liked him by how nice they were to me. One day, an attractive, sprightly blonde classmate of his named Nina Savchick let me ride her brand-new bicycle. As I happily mounted and rode away, I thought to myself, "Oh, oh, Lloyd has had it." They recently celebrated their sixtieth wedding anniversary.

Returning to school was always a shock. From Ms. Haweeli's class I went on to junior high school, where I made a raft of new friends from the other grade schools in town—some of them even girls. A few old friends from King School showed up, but I was less comfortable with them. They still liked to act tough, smoke, and take chances with the authorities, while I had moved on. However, I still occasionally hung out with them on "the corner," one of those unlikely places near my home where kids congregated for no other reason than to talk and look for trouble. Most of it involved pranks rather than lawbreaking, but the temptation to overstep was always there.

"How would you like to earn some easy money?" a close friend asked one day. He explained that he and another guy had found an unlocked window in a shed where the local grocery store stowed beer. "We're going to steal a couple of cases tonight and sell them, want to come along?" "No, I don't think that's a good idea, and you shouldn't either. You might get caught." He went ahead anyway; and after several successful heists, the shortages were discovered—and the police were waiting for them.

My friend was sent to the state reformatory school in Concord for a year. We corresponded by letter: he described life at the institution (very strict, but otherwise, not too bad), and I provided hometown news and tried to keep his spirits up. When released, our friendship resumed. He had learned a lesson and stayed out of trouble. He finished high school, went on to a teachers' college, and had an exemplary career as a secondary school teacher. Just the way the penal system was supposed to work.

Most other childhood risks were self-induced and grew out of my lifelong tendency to court danger. One was high diving, prompted by watching Captain Jimmy Jamison, the closing act in a traveling carnival that came through Berlin.

Dressed in a skintight gleaming white suit, he would climb slowly up a one-hundred-foot ladder supported only by guy wires, to stand on a tiny platform looking out into the darkness. His figure, bathed in searchlights, would remain poised and motionless, high above a small circular tank of water, while the crowd waited breathlessly for him to jump. Just as tension peaked, he would turn to face the ladder, pause, and fall back in a perfect somersault, landing in the shallow tank. The crowd would gasp, roar their approval—and make plans to return the following night.

My high-diving act was also from a ladder, but not nearly as high, although the danger might have been comparable. Several of my friends and I spent weeks selecting and chopping down tall, straight trees, and after stripping the limbs, laid them side by side, and end to end, on the ground. Then we nailed crossbars at angles, joining them together, and rungs between them to create a ladder about forty feet long. We planted one end at the edge of a remote, deep reservoir, our favorite swimming hole, and with ropes and braces and many hands, somehow managed to muscle the ladder upright and secure it in place. I began diving off at lower levels first, working my way up the swaying, rickety ladder, until the moment of truth arrived: the top.

Like Jamison, I stayed poised there, not to attract spectators but to screw up my courage—then off I jumped. Only two other friends were brave (or dumb) enough to follow me off the highest rung, giving us status among peers of the best kind. As time went on, we became more confident of our positioning in the air and in our ability to time entry into the water. We eventually added front and back somersaults to our repertoire, and I, for good measure, a full gainer. We performed whenever a suitable audience was available, defined loosely as one with at least four people (less if it included girls). There were close calls (once when a rung broke as the diver pushed off and barely made it to the water), but no injuries.

In the winter, I skated on man-made rinks, remote ponds, and for miles on the Androscoggin River, which always had open water in the middle because of a strong current. I strayed too far from shore one day, broke through the ice, and just managed to scramble out. It was a long walk home, stiff-legged and chilled to the bone in my frozen pants. "Pick up" hockey games were played on the smaller ponds, and lasted until the ice got chewed up. We ended play by chopping a hole in the middle, gathering around it, and bouncing up and down to pump water onto the ice for a new surface the next day—our version of the latter-day Zamboni.

And, of course, there was skiing. Largely because of the influx of Norwegian immigrants, the first ski club in the nation was formed in Berlin. In the 1930s and '40s, we had the highest ski jump in North America (noted for the longest jump), and hosted international competitions. I learned to ski almost as soon as I could walk. My first "real" skis (my father made an earlier pair) were made of pine, with a leather toe strap in the middle. I cut large "rubber bands" from an old inner tube, inserted my toe in the strap, and stretched the bands from heel to toe for bindings. For the first time, I was able to make downhill turns, however rudimentary. Ski lifts didn't exist, so I skied wherever a steep pasture or trail could be found, often helping to clear them on particularly inviting terrain. From that modest beginning, the sport has moved beyond a few intrepid enthusiasts on untracked hills, to family outings on groomed slopes, in massive enclaves of man-made snow. I am still an enthusiast.

One of the greatest challenges was skiing down the Headwall in Tuckerman's Ravine, high up on Mount Washington. In the winter, heavy blowing snow against a sheer cliff creates a huge bowl unsafe to ski except in late spring. It takes the better part of a day, carrying skis, poles, and boots, just to climb above the headwall—much of it so steep it is like climbing a ladder set too close to a house, with the possibility of falling backward.

"Going over the lip" and streaking down the Headwall locked in "bear trap" bindings on wooden skies, was a feat few attempted—which, of course, made it all the more appealing. I skied it as a teenager, and a few times in my fifties with my children, Jeff and Marcy, then in their teens and excellent skiers. I thought of it as a "rite of passage" for them, and a challenge for me. By the time David was ready, I was pushing sixty, and thought better of it.

Upon entering high school, I had to choose one of three courses: college preparatory, commercial or mechanical arts. I chose college preparatory—why, I don't know. No one in my family on either side had ever gone to college, and I hardly knew anyone who had. The subject never came up at home. The idea must have been sparked by Ms. Haweeli, or my peers in her class—certainly not from neighborhood friends. It was a critical choice.

"College Preps" were a distinct minority in Berlin High School, less than forty students in my class of two hundred and twenty. We were out of the mainstream of student life, neither envied nor admired, just looked at differently. Relations with old friends in other majors became a bit awkward, and I began to wonder if I had made a mistake, until I noticed that teachers also looked at us differently—with a little more respect, certainly higher expectations, and often with more personal interest. It wasn't long before we began to think we were pretty special.

The curriculum included higher math, French, and Latin, along with all the basic sciences, further setting us apart. To my surprise, I excelled in Latin and loved it, while struggling mightily with French (my low point was declining the verb "pleuer" when called on, which translated into "I rain," "you rain," "we rain," while the class howled). The pace was fast, homework extensive, and goals were high. The small class size fostered strong relationships, and a certain mutual pride. Several became lifelong friends, like Ike Morrison, a Jewish kid, and Lionel Marois of French Canadian decent, who were classmates through college and ushered in my wedding and I in theirs. We still get together almost every year.

Summer jobs were considered a necessity in our family, although our parents never pressed us to help support ourselves; we simply wanted to because they were working so hard to "make ends meet." Too young to get "working papers" for a "real" job, I settled for the lowly position of "Cookee" for a construction crew on the top of Mount Washington. I met the crew at 6:00 a.m. each Monday morning, clambered into the back of a truck, was driven fourteen miles to the foot of the mountain and eight miles more to the 6,200-foot summit—and back again Friday afternoons. We were building a test facility for the army air force. The job didn't pay much, but it was exciting to be up there, especially in bad weather.

I peeled potatoes, set and cleared tables, and washed dishes for the cook, a thoughtful, self-educated Scotsman who had held a series of white-collar jobs before being reduced to the present one. Despite the age gap, we got on well together, and talked of many things. He imparted the usual adult-to-youth bromides, a few great truths, and unconsciously, one lasting lesson: the importance of avoiding the mind-numbing "might have beens" in life—those paths not taken because of timidity or indecision. He had become paralyzed by the things he wished he had done, and was unable to tackle things he still hoped to do. I vowed not to make the same mistake, instead, to commit and then make it work.

When I reached sixteen later that summer, I sought and found a higher paying job: as railroad section hand, a "gandy dancer," working about thirty miles from Berlin. My commute was on a caboose hitched to a freight train leaving home Sunday evenings and returning the following Friday. I really had no idea what a gandy dancer did except work outside and get a reasonable paycheck plus room and board. I arrived to find I had joined a rough, tough crew, with language to match, sleeping and eating in converted railroad boxcars on a siding near Bethel, Maine. Our job was to replace rotted ties, worn rails, and washed-out roadbeds along a forty-mile stretch—all manual labor of the least challenging kind. I was shoveling away on my first day when the foreman, a big man with a lantern jaw, sidled up to me, and said, "Take it easy, kid, don't work so hard." Thinking he was being sarcastic, I shoveled even faster. He pulled me aside, and said, "Listen, kid, I mean it. When we git to the end of this section, we jes start back again. We been doing this for a long time, and we ain't in no hurry."

They were all much older than I, with the exception of a red-headed Irishman in his mid-twenties who, it turned out, had a criminal record. We became friendly, and had long discussions on a variety of subjects while working. I was fascinated by his stories about prison life and turbulent background, and found him quite bright. I urged him to get an education and "go straight." He never argued the point; he just never agreed to try. When I said good-bye to him in September, I had the uneasy feeling that nothing was going to change. I never saw or heard of him again.

Back in school for my junior year, it was a full academic load and a rekindled desire to be a star athlete. I had been playing on the basketball and football junior varsity teams and making some progress, but my true talent was still largely undiscovered. This was to be my year. The basic problem, however, was that most of my contemporaries had gotten their postmaturation growth while I was still waiting for mine, and I lacked the athletic ability to make up for it. I did, however, become a starting forward in basketball, despite being about five feet six inches tall and weighing 120 pounds.

Freddie Bockman, the other starting forward, was not much taller, and we became known as the "mighty midgets" in local press accounts—not exactly the accolade I had in mind. However, I grew taller in my senior year, and the team made it to the state tournament where we were competitive but not victorious. Freddie joined the navy after graduation and was lost in the Pacific when his ship was sunk shortly afterward. Gene Gothreau, another varsity teammate, also joined the navy and was killed in action. Even as an invincible teenager, I found it sobering that two starting teammates out of five failed to make it to their twentieth birthdays.

In football, my size condemned me to a second-string quarterback's role, despite my determination. But I loved it anyway. I remember feeling ten feet tall when encased in a leather helmet, thick shoulder, thigh, and hip pads, and ankle-high cleated shoes. We practiced on a cinder field every afternoon until dusk in the frosty temperatures of northern New Hampshire, and then hiked a mile or so back to the locker room, bruised, scraped, and exhilarated. Alas, I barely made the team, scored no touchdowns, and in fact, seldom got into games. The closest I came to scoring was once when on the opponent's three-yard line and far ahead, I was sent in to fake a pass and run off tackle. As we broke from the huddle, my teammates exhorted each other to "open a big hole for 'Chobe.'" And they did, except as I started through the hole, a big hand appeared from nowhere and stopped me in my tracks. Just one hand!

Perhaps the most memorable event in my football career was standing on the stage before a high-school assembly while the coach praised my spirit and hard work despite my lack of size (and success). The ceremony was meant to encourage more boys to go out for football, while to me it was more like being the fat Boy Scout cited as "the most improved" at whatever. But it didn't really matter; I was just happy to be able to play.

The next summer, I worked at the Mount Washington Hotel; coincidentally, where my mother and father first met. I "walloped" pots, washed dishes, and peeled vegetables in the massive kitchen for more than ten hours a day, seven days a week, for thirty-five dollars a month—and considered myself lucky. Although we worked hard, there was much to do during our time off, and a great many young people (especially waitresses) to do it with. Now recently restored to its original grandeur, I dined at the hotel with my family this past winter, and my son David arranged an escorted tour around the kitchen with the tuxedo-clad maitre d'. David had listened ad nauseam to my stories over the years about "when I was a boy, I worked so hard, etc.," that he wanted to see where I slaved. I'm afraid he didn't think it looked all that bad.

As I entered my senior year, I began thinking about what to do after graduation. These days, when parents are constantly planning, preparing, and exhorting their kids to work hard and build a résumé to gain acceptance in a "good" college, it is difficult to believe how remote a college education was at that time. As mentioned earlier, the subject never came up at my house, and as far as I know, wasn't even considered by my brothers and sister. My father's advice was to finish high school, learn a trade, and then "we could always get a job." My sister was expected to find a husband.

Fortunately, that college preparatory course and my basketball prowess came together at the state tournament at the University of New Hampshire in Durham, when I visited my first college and realized for the first time that I too might become a college student. I peppered an older former football teammate, then a freshman, with questions on college courses, schedules, and homework, and costs for tuition, room, and board. And suddenly, it seemed possible, and I decided to apply. The decision of where was easy. The University of New Hampshire was the only college I'd seen, and probably the only one I could afford—and I knew I would have to pay for it.

I had always saved a portion of my earnings from all jobs, but the "big" money was made during the summers. I had accumulated almost a hundred dollars working at the Mount Washington Hotel which, when added to savings from the cookee and gandy dancer jobs, totaled a little more than two hundred dollars—enough for tuition ($150) and first semester's room and board. I filled out an application, arranged transcripts, and was accepted. My parents were largely uninvolved in the process. They had had no experience with higher education and little appreciation for its effect on my future. Although I know they hoped I would do well, I'm not sure they thought it was a good idea. There were no emotional partings, overt expressions of pride, or last-minute admonitions to work hard and write often. To spare them a long drive to Durham (approximately four hours each way), I simply packed up, said good-bye, and hitched a ride with a friend and his father.

Those first days at the university were marked by the usual blur of activity: finding my dorm, meeting a new roommate, signing up for courses, and for some of us, finding a part-time job. It was exciting, challenging, and relatively painless. Being away from home was not new. With a few high-school friends to share the experience, the transition was quite comfortable. That is, until we started student orientation.

I was surprised to find my "Activities Schedule" significantly different from that of my friends, notably for gym and other athletic activities. Confused, I checked further and found I had been assigned the women's schedule. After explaining to more than a few people that this Sherley (spelled with an *e*) was male, I got it straightened out, but not before the student names and gender had been circulated to the assigned classrooms. The inevitable embarrassments at class roll calls commenced. The instructor would call a Ms. Adams, for example, and a feminine voice would respond "Here." Then Mr. Brown, answered by "Here" in a low masculine voice, and so on, until he reached my name. "Ms. Rines," he would call. I would slump in my seat and reply "Here" in the deepest voice I could muster. It always got a laugh, but unfortunately at my expense.

Career plans were hazy at best. I knew only that I didn't want to work for someone else. Even the word "job" had a chilling connotation, especially when connected to companies or products with little excitement or redeeming value. I remember wondering how anyone could choose a career selling soap, for example, as did many graduates working for Proctor and Gamble. I was idealistic enough to think that I had loftier goals: independence, helping mankind, and—a personal mantra—*success on my terms; money is less important than career satisfaction.*

Most of those conditions were met in professions—particularly, medicine. Although intrigued but not passionate about the idea, I considered electing a premed major. But there was a war going on, and like most men my age, I was anxious to serve. And then I knew exactly what I wanted to do: fly. Because of the soaring demand for doctors, premed students were either deferred from military service or called in and educated at government expense. Either way, it would preclude aviation training. The solution, worked out with my faculty advisor, was a customized program avoiding the declaration of "Premed," but including most of its courses, leaving time for electives in meteorology and higher math to enhance my chances of being selected for flight training. I would preserve the option of pursuing medicine after the war.

The resulting course load was heavy but manageable; Berlin High School's college preparatory program had, in fact, prepared me well for college work. I quickly analyzed the time and effort each course would likely require for specific grades, confident I could get an A in any course if I wanted it badly enough. Because being a "grind" was not my style, nor that of my peer group, I targeted levels high enough to make the dean's list and graduate cum laude, and then proceeded to enjoy college life.

My schedule evolved into the usual routine of classes, study, part-time work, dating, and beer drinking. I was elected president of my dormitory, a position with few duties and no prerogatives, but one that provided sufficient visibility to put me high on the "rush" list of fraternities. I chose Kappa Sigma, then considered a "jock house" with a big-man-on-campus aura (we thought), and I was elected president of my twenty-member pledge class. This in turn led to my nomination in a two-student race for president of the six-hundred-member class of '46. Election protocol at that time did not countenance campaigning in any form. In fact, nominees were expected to appear indifferent to the election outcome despite an obvious desire for the honor. I apparently feigned indifference too well. I lost—to a cheerleader!

Part 2

WORLD WAR II

On December 7, 1941, the "day that will live in infamy," America's destiny was determined, and its role defined for the twentieth century and beyond. I couldn't know then that my life was similarly in play, poised on the high-wire of disaster. Still in high school, the world in flames, and the outcome uncertain, choices with enormous consequences had to be made. While many friends were burdened by irresolution or worse, I saw opportunity and more. Writ large, of course, was the chance to fly for the armed services.

Too young to be threatened by the draft, yet old enough to "sign up for the duration," I aimed for the top: naval aviation. That decision and its successful pursuit unfold in the next two years, culminating in the gold wings of a naval aviator, an officer's commission, and selection for fighter-pilot training.

CHAPTER 3

REALIZING A DREAM

Pretty coeds, parties, football games, and interesting courses—all the ingredients were there for a happy college experience. But it was the fall of 1942, only nine months after Pearl Harbor, and war was raging around the world. The draft was in full swing for twenty-one-year-olds, and was certain to go lower. At just eighteen, however, there was little reason to be concerned, but I was anxious to serve anyway. I decided to stay in school long enough to decide which service had the best training program and then apply. Flying, of course, was my dream. I had read about it for years, hung around local airports, and done everything but go up in an airplane. Here was the opportunity to pursue that dream, and perhaps, the ultimate fulfillment: the gold wings of a navy fighter pilot.

Most male students were in similar situations but few of them knew what to do. So the university designated a professor to study the array of educational deferment opportunities offered by the military services, weigh the likely advantages in each, and advise students accordingly. Professor Thut was selected for this unenviable task, and did his best to fathom the unfathomable in the nation's chaotic mobilization programs. His considered conclusion was that the army's Enlisted Reserve Corps, which only accepted college students, would provide the longest deferment, and when activated, the best chance for assignment to officer-candidate school. The vast majority of male students accepted this advice and signed up. I had other ideas.

I telephoned the navy department in Boston "cold," and was transferred several times before reaching the appropriate department. After listening to a brief recitation of my background and goals, the officer described their V-5 Program for pilot training, the general physical and educational qualifications required, and the process for applying and meeting the requirements. I asked for the earliest appointment available to take the mental and physical exams, and was given a date three weeks later. Then I told my friend "Butch" Marois about the program, and he immediately called and got an appointment for the same day, hoping we could go into the navy together.

We arrived in Boston the night before the scheduled date, checked into a hotel, and planned an early dinner and retirement to be well rested for the next day's tests. That is, until I broached the idea of going to the famous "Old Howard" to see a burlesque show, a first for both of us. A long and hard debate ensued, largely out of concern for the navy's notoriously stringent eye examinations, covering depth perception, color discrimination, and direct and peripheral visual acuity.

This was serious business. Would the bright lights strain our eyes? What about watching swirling, lightly clad chorus girls too intently? Would we be staying up too late? Would we be too tired? We finally agreed: "To hell with it, let's go and take our chances." It was a memorable show, one most of our peers would never see—and our vision the next morning was never sharper! The theater closed shortly afterward, and Scolly Square and the Old Howard were replaced by an uninspiring government center. I had avoided one more of those "might-have-beens." in life, however inconsequential.

We arrived at the navy's 150 Causeway Street building promptly at 8:00 a.m., and spent a full day taking exams. The intelligence tests were comprehensive, challenging, and exhaustive, and took up most of the morning. Then came the interminable wait to learn if I had qualified to take the physicals. When called in to see the officer in charge, he told me I had passed and added casually, "Your scores couldn't have been much higher." Thus heartened, I went on to the physical and psychological exams, spending the afternoon being punctured, probed, and x-rayed, and finally, tested and interviewed in-depth by a psychiatrist. We both passed, and were told we would be called up as soon as a billet was available. I was walking on air.

One more detail had to be addressed, however. As a student in a land-grant university, I had been required to enroll in the Reserve Officers Training Corps and be sworn into the U.S. Army. I couldn't be in the navy too. When I explained the situation to the ROTC commander, and showed him my official acceptance in the Navy, he said: "You'll have to continue in the ROTC and remain in the army, but when called up by the navy you can resign." Almost as an afterthought, he wrote on my army records: HOLD FOR THE NAVY in big red letters.

A few weeks later, just after the second semester began, we awoke to news that the Enlisted Reserve Corps had been activated, and its members ordered to report for active duty immediately. Instantly, homework assignments were discarded, classes cut, and college life ended for most of the male students on campus. Those of us not called watched with a mixture of relief and sadness as the stunned new soldiers-to-be packed up and disappeared. Although some made it to officer-candidate schools, most of them were sent to basic-training camps, and dispersed as enlisted men to combat theaters around the world, not to return, even on furlough, until war's end. Some never returned.

Collectively, they became known as "Thut's Lost Battalion," victims of the good professor's well meant but errant advice. Sadly, some of them had signed up for other services, as I had, and sighing with relief, continued going to classes. Within weeks, they were notified by the army that they were "Absent Without Leave," and ordered to report forthwith. They had failed to get that big red "HOLD" on their records, and were activated, without recourse. I had quite literally "dodged a bullet"—and preserved a dream.

Everything changed. Close friends were no longer there, athletic teams were decimated, and classes and dining halls were sparsely attended. Even partying lost some of its luster, although I couldn't help appreciating the vastly improved ratio of girls to boys. The remainder of that school year was subdued as the war news worsened, and mobilization continued apace. The draft age was progressively lowered, finally reaching deep down in the eighteen-year-old pool, as the net widened to include childless married men, and eventually, those with children. The pervasive tragedy of war was spreading.

My brother Stan had followed my dad's advice and become a machinist working in a war industry. Still in his early twenties, he was the first in our family to be drafted. It was a major event with good-byes, moist eyes, and a boisterous send-off by friends at the local railroad station. After basic training in the army, he was assigned to a unit to escort and guard prisoners of war, both in the United States and Europe, and eventually attended the University of Kansas, where he earned a year's college credits by war's end.

He added two more years at the University of New Hampshire and joined Kappa Sigma fraternity, so we became brothers twice over. The entrepreneur of the family, he created a company called Container Research to build highly engineered reusable containers. Today, they have hundreds of employees in two plants, building containers for aircraft engines, helicopter blades, missiles, and other items too highly classified to describe—all possible because he learned a trade.

Lloyd, deferred first as a married man and then as a father when daughter Carole was born, wasn't drafted until early 1944. He was trained in communications, and sent to Europe just in time to be swept up in the Battle of the Bulge and spend months in torrid combat until the Germans surrendered in May of 1945. He returned home, joined a consumer finance company, and in time, became president of the largest commercial bank in the North Country.

My sister Gerry fulfilled her patriotic duty by resigning a secretarial position to take a "Rosie the Riveter" type job in Hartford. She returned to Berlin after the war, married an owner/manager of several restaurants, for whom she did secretarial work while raising a family.

At the end of my freshman year, I applied for a job at the Brown Company. The employment office was crowded with applicants that day, and each of us was asked to submit a brief written description of our work and educational background. To my surprise, although I was almost last in line, my name was called first. "Because you've been to college," the interviewer told me—the first real-life example showing the value of a college education. I was hired as a laborer.

My job was to assist "millwrights," essentially utility men dispatched to whatever part of the mill was in need of help. I was shocked to find myself working alongside and doing much the same work on my first day as many in the crew had been doing for years. Some of the men were quite intelligent, capable of more challenging occupations, and longed for greater opportunities where few were available; while others were simply resigned to their fate, content to exchange eight hours of their life each day for a paycheck. When one fellow worker learned I was going to college, he said rather poignantly, "I wish I had your future."

The wait for orders from the navy was almost more than I could bear. Each day's mail arrival was an event I either attended in person or checked on by telephone, as did Marois, for we expected to be called in together. By midsummer, most of my friends were in the service, many of them long enough to return home on leave, resplendent in uniforms, and loaded with tales of their military and travel experiences. I envied them, and became increasingly uncomfortable in civilian clothes, suggesting a 4-F rejection for military service for a mélange of reasons, none of them good. But above all, I ached with impatience to start flying.

In early August, I received an excited call from my friend, saying he had received orders to report to a naval air station in Iowa. He was ecstatic, as was I, confident that my orders would be in the same mail. But there was no letter that day. I even trekked to the post office to see if one had arrived too late to be delivered. None had. Surely I would receive one the next day. I didn't. I was devastated.

Soon after he left, letters arrived describing his role as TARMAC, instead of aviation cadet as expected. Essentially, he was called to replace workers fueling and working around airplanes, while waiting for a place in the cadet program.

Although not flying, it seemed a lot more attractive than marking time in Berlin, and prompted yet another phone call to 150 Causeway, eliciting only routine responses and no specific information.

In utter frustration, I decided to go to Boston on the slim chance of getting to see someone, anyone, to shed light on my situation, and perhaps move things along. The reception was neither warm nor accommodating, and I was bounced around to several offices before I reached the desk of a knowledgeable and somewhat sympathetic lieutenant. After listening to my story, he understood my frustration and was explaining why it was taking so long, when his phone rang.

He listened quietly for a moment, then put his hand over the phone, and said, "One of the cadets due to start this Thursday"—three days away—"has had an emergency appendectomy, do you want to take his place?" I blurted an excited, "Yes." He gave the caller my name and hung up. I was euphoric, especially when told I would leapfrog TARMAC duty, and go directly to flight preparatory school at Williams College as an *aviation cadet*.

With orders in hand, I hurried home to inform my parents, who tried unsuccessfully to share my joy, while concealing concern. There was little to do before leaving. I was ordered to take only personal items and the clothes I was wearing. Call-ups had become so common that "going off to war" was a nonevent, hardly noticed by friends and associates. In my excitement, my parents' anguish at having another son, especially the youngest, leave home never occurred to me. On Thursday, I drove my father back to work after lunch before my departure on the 2:30 train. It was a quiet ride with some last-minute admonitions and advice. As we stood by the car to say good-bye, he gave me a brief hug, and I noted his eyes were glistening and saw a tear trickle down his cheek, something I had never seen before. As I write this, more than a half century later, the memory is as clear, and the unspoken emotions as intense, as they were then— only the trickling tear is now mine.

After two days of swearing in, physical exams, and filling out forms at a base in South Boston, twenty-five of us, still in civilian clothes, were marched in a ragtag formation through the streets to North Station. No one paid any attention to us; this too had long since become commonplace. After a five-hour train ride, we arrived in Williamstown, the home of Williams College, in the dead of night. We were met at the railroad station by a tall, athletic officer named Ensign Krick who, bathed in floodlights, ordered us to "Fall in, line up, and stand at attention." Then, after a string of instructions, he closed with the stentorian pronouncement, "You are in the navy now and you will do what I tell you to do." He meant it. Tough but fair, he was our platoon officer for the next four months, riding herd on everything we did, said, or, in time, thought.

We were assigned eight to a room designed for two college students. Routed out at five thirty the next morning, we were marched through a bewildering schedule beginning with the regulation two-minute haircut (no scissors, no sideburns, and almost, no hair) and then to the supply rooms, where we were issued "uniforms." Instead of the snappy blue cadet uniforms we envisioned, or crisp freshly pressed khakis, we were handed Civilian Conservation Corps clothes left over from Depression days. Made of heavy green cloth, ill-fitting, and designed for rough wear, the only navy insignia was a patch with V-5 and embroidered gold wings on my "overseas" cap.

This was "Flight Preparatory School," four months of ground school, with heavy doses of military and physical training. The courses ranged from aerodynamics, aircraft engines, and meteorology, to naval history, military etiquette, and the all-encompassing NAVY REGULATIONS. We also began a never-ending training program in communications, learning to send and receive messages in Morse code, semaphore, and blinkers at ever increasing speeds. And we were introduced to a course simply named "Recognition," to recognize virtually all enemy planes and ships in a fiftieth of a second flash, and instantly recall their vital statistics—to determine who to attack and how. I doubted it possible to recognize anything at that speed, and memorize all that information. It turned out to be simple—by incessant rote and repetition for months on end.

Sitting in a darkened room, staring unblinkingly at a large screen, the instructor intoned "Ready," "Now," and then flashed a five-digit number lasting a tenth of a second. As instructed, I immediately tried to write it down. The first three digits I was sure of, the fourth I thought I knew, and the fifth was a wild guess. We tried it again, and again, and again, and by the end of the class, were reaching for six digits, flashed at slightly higher speeds. It was a class given several times a week at every base throughout the two-year program.

I gradually progressed to eight digits at ever increasing speed, then to actual photographs of Japanese and German planes and warships, and learned the length, wingspan, armament, cruising, and top speeds of each plane, and comparable statistics for each vessel. By graduation, I could stare at that screen, listen to the measured words "Ready," "Now," and recognize every object in a fiftieth of a second. In that same instant, those vital statistics would pop into my mind ready to be calibrated in a gun sight. Amazing.

We were pushed to the limit in daily calisthenics, diabolically designed obstacle courses, and aggressive competitive sports, all inevitably topped off with a long-distance run, in uniform, in formation on Saturday afternoons. Ensign Krick marched us everywhere, yelled at us constantly, and watched our every move. But always with a certain amount of respect: foul language was never used or tolerated, discipline was measured but sure, and excellence in all intellectual and physical activities was demanded. Gradually, the idea seeped into our consciences that we might be special, destined to do great things. I couldn't have been happier.

Weekends consisted of "liberty" on Saturday afternoons, mandatory chapel attendance Sunday morning, and free time in the afternoon and evening. There wasn't much to do except go to the movies or wander around Williamstown, and occasionally, visit North Adams, a larger town a few miles down the road. On my first foray to North Adams, I happened to meet an army colonel walking the opposite direction, and gave him a smart salute—my first off the base. He seemed startled, gave me a token salute in return, and walked on. A few minutes later, a car pulled up, and the colonel rolled down a window and called me over. I must have looked scared, for he quickly said, "Don't worry, it's okay. I just want to know what the devil service you're in, wearing a uniform like that." When I told him, he shook his head and drove on; no doubt with the army's traditional dim view of the navy reinforced.

In many ways, Williams College was as unlikely a setting for military training as it was beautiful, but it solved many of the problems of wartime training while "staying in business." It provided excellent facilities and accomplished faculty for training aviation cadets and other officer candidates at a time when civilian students were a rarity. Mobilization had drained the nation's campuses, especially those with all-male students like Williams, leaving their facilities underused, and tuition income drastically reduced. By using those college campuses for military training, the government kept them financially viable and the faculty employed, preserving these institutions until war's end.

By December, the four-month curriculum had been completed, and twenty-one of my original twenty-five-man platoon had survived. Four were "washed out" for academic or disciplinary reasons, and sent to boot camp in Bainbridge, Maryland, a place that gradually took on the dread sound of "Alcatraz" for by this time we had received cadet uniforms, and had begun to think of ourselves as officers and gentlemen. For those who didn't make it, Bainbridge and the change to enlisted status—bell-bottom trousers and dashed hopes of flying—was devastating. Washing out of a program requiring such special skills was no disgrace, but to the cadet's friends and family, however couched, it inevitably connoted failure.

The next step was war training school at Keene, New Hampshire, only about one hundred miles away, but an all-day train ride for us. Passenger trains were still crisscrossing the country, connecting small towns and large cities alike, and because they burned coal instead of rationed gasoline, the armed services used them whenever possible. It was a pleasant if slow trip, watching the countryside slide past while listening to conductors announce stations I'd never heard of, located in towns found on few maps.

We were greeted upon arrival by a rather plump professor, dressed in a black suit with brass buttons, trying to look like a naval officer. He immediately lined us up, and marched us several blocks through the center of town. Keene Teacher's

College looked like anything but a military facility with its colonial architecture, quiet setting, and lazy pace. There were only a handful of navy personnel to order us around, so we were treated more like students than cadets by the civilian teachers. Half of each day was devoted to ground school, consisting of much the same curriculum followed at Williams, but with a few added subjects on actual flying, and only a smattering of physical activities. Not very demanding or particularly illuminating, but it didn't matter—we were there to learn how TO FLY.

Once again organized into twenty-five-men platoons, we alternated weekly between mornings and afternoons of flight training and ground school. The airfield was about a fifteen-minute bus trip away, and consisted of a hangar, and a low-slung wooden administration building and pilots' lounge, located beside a short grass airstrip. Not very different from the airport I hung around near Berlin. What *was* different, though, was the fifteen or so bright yellow Piper Cubs available for us to fly.

As mentioned earlier, I had never been up in an airplane, much less flown one, so just looking at them made my heart pump faster. We were there to learn the rudiments of flying—in effect, to get the equivalent of a private pilot's license—and were to be trained by civilian flight instructors. But first we had to learn how to start the engine—not just what switch to turn on and when, but how to spin the propeller by hand to get the engine to fire. Just as Johnny West had done earlier, it was right out of a grade-B aviation movie, the ones that enthralled me as a kid. The cadet assigned to spin the propeller would await the sequential commands of "Switch off," "Switch on," and "Contact," repeating each in a loud and clear voice, before pulling the prop through with a special follow-through motion, moving himself away from the whirling propeller when the engine caught. The procedure and technique, however ritualistic, was always carefully followed. Being hit by a prop was usually fatal—a fact impressed upon us frequently.

My first flight was not the exquisite event I anticipated, probably because I was too busy trying to remember all I had been taught and still listen to my instructor's running comments. He was a tall slender man in pro forma leather jacket and sunglasses, somewhere in his late thirties. He always appeared lethargic and bored, until I did something—anything—wrong. Then he erupted verbally and physically, emphasizing his words by slamming his fist on the instrument panel. His reaction was unsettling, to say the least, especially if I happened to be dealing with a missed approach or bad landing. About the only redeeming feature of this technique was the relief I felt when, midway in the fifth hour of flight, he climbed out of the plane at the end of the runway, and said laconically, "You take it around."

I still remember how different the plane flew without him and how many new and strange noises emanated from the engine—sounds that I had never noticed before. But I was soloing and had that special satisfaction of being in complete control of the aircraft without anyone coaching me. After flying around the area for five or ten minutes, I made several successful landings, presumably under his watchful eye. But when I taxied in, anticipating some kind of commentary or maybe a pat on the back, he had left for the day. In a way, that may have been the greatest compliment of all, and probably the surest sign that I was now a real pilot.

On subsequent flights, he took me through various controlled maneuvers, such as figure 8s, wingovers, stalls, and tailspins. I was amazed and pleased to find how tasks that seemed almost impossible to do at first became so easy so soon. As the New Hampshire winter closed in on us, frigid temperatures and snow gradually became significant hazards. Just getting a plane started for an early morning flight was a major accomplishment. The engine would be so cold that we could "chin" ourselves on the propeller and it wouldn't move. It took two cadets to rotate it the first time, and as much as an hour of pulling it through before it was loose enough to spin.

The Piper Cub was fabric covered, had no heater, and cold air poured in around the windows and door. I often sat up there at twenty degrees below zero for an hour or more, listening, learning, and practicing. Despite "long john" underwear, heavy socks, woodsman boots, and whatever sweaters and jackets I could manage to pile on, I would land chilled to the bone. And then the snow became so deep the planes had to be fitted with skis, and I had to learn new techniques for takeoffs and landings. The Northerners among us managed to tolerate the cold and snow; the Southerners couldn't believe it.

Keene, in its quiet academic setting, seemed a long way from the war and the battles being fought around the world. One evening, it was all brought closer when a decorated former fighter pilot, home on leave, was asked to address us. He certainly looked the part, with his crushed cap, silk scarf, and leather flight jacket. He matter-of-factly recounted several hair-raising tales of combat against the "Japs" in the China Theater as part of the famed "Flying Tigers," a volunteer group of U.S. military pilots organized by General Chenault before America entered the war. Flying obsolete P-40 Tomahawks, they were outgunned and outmaneuvered by the faster Japanese Zeros, but still managed to hold their own.

He recounted downing several Zeros and being shot down himself, and aided by Chinese peasants, returning to fight again. He was still in his early twenties. We found it all fascinating and very romantic, until one cadet raised his hand, and said, "Sir, I've read that some Japanese pilots shot American pilots while they helplessly floated down in parachutes. What did the Flying Tigers do when they saw a Japanese pilot bail out?" We all expected a ringing tribute to American gallantry and fair play. He paused, and then said, quietly but evenly, "It would be sort of a race to see who could get to him first." The room suddenly became very quiet—and the war seemed much closer.

Ground school and flight training continued apace with little time to think and less to play. Each flight was graded by the instructor, and discussed afterward on the ground. We learned to master the stalls and tailspins, and learned the rudiments of flying on instruments. Check flights were flown periodically with the only real naval aviator at the school, an older, heavier, and immensely bored full lieutenant who obviously aspired to more exciting duty. Every now and then a cadet would fail to make the grade and be sent to Bainbridge, never to be seen or heard from again. This happened to seven out of our twenty-five-man platoon. For the rest of us, our flying ability continued to improve, but not as rapidly as our burgeoning self-confidence.

My own dangerous hubris was brought home to me one day when I elected to fly through, rather than around, a snow squall. I had not flown on instruments before, and became momentarily disoriented. To add to the discomfort, heavy turbulence was encountered, and I began to lose all sense of whether I was climbing or diving, or banking right or left, when I suddenly broke out of the clouds and found the ground off to my side instead of below me. That brief brush with real danger and incipient panic taught me the perils of over confidence. And it made me a believer in the old airman's warning that "a pilot will never be as good again as he thinks he is with forty hours' flying time under his belt." It was one of the reasons so many new pilots failed to become old ones.

After completing the flight syllabus and ground-school requirements in early April, I had earned the equivalent of a private pilot's license, and was ready for the next phase: preflight school at the University of North Carolina, at Chapel Hill. Although in name and concept it appeared almost redundant to flight preparatory school at Williams, it was a world apart in execution. From the moment we arrived, we were organized, directed, instructed, and disciplined by professional navy personnel. Reveille at 0530, beds made, room cleaned, and inspection passed, before "falling in" and being marched off to breakfast at 0630. Return to room at 0730, and prepare for class or physical activity at 0800. Thereafter, every minute of every day was scheduled until Taps at 2200, when lights went out and silence reigned. There were no exceptions, no allowances for individual deficiencies, and no excuses. And everyone had to be ON TIME, all the time.

The penalty for infractions, graded by importance, was calibrated in blocks of five demerits with one hour of extra duty (marching back and forth with a rifle) on the following Saturday afternoon—during the cadet's precious free time. Even the smallest infraction—an unsatisfactorily shined shoe, failure to pass a white-glove room inspection, or minor tardiness—was assigned five demerits. Multiples of five demerits with commensurate hours of extra duty were handed down as the level of offenses rose. Fifty demerits during the four-month program, and you were gone, washed out, and on your way to Bainbridge. And because officers steeped in military discipline were in charge, there were no appeals, no second chances.

I amassed thirty demerits and those interminable six hours of solitary marching in the first month for a series of minor offenses. Five demerits were for being *one second* late (measured on a stopwatch) for a scheduled activity, and another five when I was heard complaining about it to roommates that night after lights out. I finally got the message and learned to conform. I never got another one.

Most of our instructors, in classrooms and on playing fields, were young, talented, and enthusiastic naval officers. The University of North Carolina grounds and facilities were extensive and extraordinarily well maintained, and the navy-supplied professional athletic equipment was of the highest quality. Cost, obviously, was not a factor. We were clothed, fed, and treated as something special, and most of us responded accordingly. Morale was high for it was hard to imagine a healthier physical and intellectual regimen. We were organized into football, basketball, and baseball teams, fully equipped and well coached, often by recognized professionals from civilian life. Wrestling, hand-to-hand combat, and boxing were given special emphasis, the latter under the tutelage of a former middleweight champion. And, of course, there were the obstacle courses, calisthenics, rope climbing, and running, supervised by trainers with stopwatches and clipboards at the ready, like appendages, exhorting us to go faster, higher, or longer. Appetites reached peak levels for food that was wholesome, hearty, and abundant, and served with a special gusto by Italian prisoners of war. Few of them spoke English, but all of them understood and responded to the word "seconds."

Italian POWs were an especially happy lot for their war was now over, and they were safely ensconced in America. Most of them were probably housed and fed better than at any time in their lives. We felt no animosity toward them, except perhaps on drill afternoons when we saw them lying down on a grassy knoll, lazily watching us, their victors, sweating it out in the hot sun.

After four months of training, I felt ready for anything. I had been examined, measured, timed, and challenged emotionally, physically, and intellectually. Along with courses in hand-to-hand combat, I had learned survival techniques the hard way by spending three days alone in surrounding forests. I even had classes on relaxation and stress management that seemed ridiculous at the time, but which proved most helpful in the years to come. Ever since, I have considered my physical condition at Chapel Hill as a benchmark for good health, exercising daily and never letting my weight stray more than five pounds from what I euphemistically call my "fighting weight."

Twenty-two of our reconstituted platoon of twenty-five graduated—an excellent record. But there was no time to relax. The failure rate would soar in the next phase, primary flight school, which was designed to begin separating ordinary pilots from the ranks of accomplished naval aviators. As it turned out in too many cases, this process was done unfairly.

CHAPTER 4

WINGS OF GOLD

I arrived at Naval Air Station Grosse Ilse, just outside of Detroit, in the spring of 1944, and was assigned to yet another platoon of twenty-five cadets, some from Chapel Hill, most from other preflight schools around the country. Although I had been in the service almost a year, it was my first experience at a real navy base with its armed guards, barracks, mess halls, and flight line. The grounds were well cared for, buildings freshly painted, and the interiors uniformly pristine. And the base was literally throbbing with the sound of planes taking off and landing, all day and into the night.

It was also the end of personal privacy. We slept in row upon row of double bunks, each flanked by footlockers containing all our worldly possessions, neatly and precisely stowed according to regulation. "Heads" and showers were wide open, and we ate in loud, cavernous mess halls. Navy personnel in uniform were everywhere, purposefully going about their routines; civilians were nowhere to be seen. I remember reflecting briefly (and proudly) on the number of people and enormous amounts of money dedicated to train so few of us to fly.

Primary Flight was an intense, comprehensive program designed not just to train us to pilot an airplane but to create naval aviators knowledgeable in all aspects of flight. Along with continuing courses in meteorology, aerodynamics, and communications in ground school, celestial navigation and dead reckoning were introduced. And in the air, the mantra was "know everything about your airplane, understand what it can do, and then do it—with precision." I was issued my own flight gear for the first time: helmet and goggles, flight jacket, flight suit, deerskin gloves, and the pièce de résistance, a long white silk scarf discretely monogrammed with the letters USN. We were even assigned our own parachutes, and for the first time, officially called pilots. My fantasy flights in a World War I "Spad" were about to be surpassed by real-life events, complete with that silk scarf, figuratively streaming from an open cockpit. "G-8" paled in comparison.

We were scheduled to fly Stearman N2Ss (a.k.a. "Yellow Perils"), a biplane with two open cockpits connected by a "gosport" tube through which to communicate. The plane had a large radial engine and a heavy propeller that enlisted men cranked to start. We were clearly getting up in the world. Each of us was assigned an instructor, a naval aviator well trained for his job. Mine was a lieutenant, junior grade, in his early twenties, who was crisp and clear in his instruction, and an excellent pilot to emulate. The first few flights were used to familiarize ourselves with the airplane, and the first solo was early and uneventful. Then we proceeded along a syllabus, pages long, that included almost every maneuver known to man. There were figure 8s, slow rolls, snap rolls, loops, tailspins, inverted tailspins, split Ss, and more, all to be executed at prescribed and precise altitudes and speeds.

The most challenging maneuvers were slow rolls and inverted spins where much of the time was spent upside down, struggling to manipulate controls while hanging from a safety belt, in the wind, with nothing between me and the ground thousands of feet below. At any time, on every flight, the instructor would simulate an emergency by snapping the throttle back and announcing that the engine had just quit. The student was expected to select a field, plan an upwind approach, and execute an emergency landing without power. The instructor would watch and wait until the student was close enough to the ground to judge if a successful landing would be made before shoving the throttle forward, climbing out, and announcing his verdict.

About halfway through the syllabus, I embarked on my first night flight—an experience that had to be lived to believe. The first hurdle was to find the plane in the dark and inspect it. Next, was to taxi along dimly lit paths to a large circular landing pad of cement, bathed in floodlights, and take off into a dark void. Without stars and few lights, the world up there consisted of blinking red and green wing lights, and flaming exhaust stacks, constantly moving in no discernible pattern. All I was instructed to do was take off, circle the field a couple of times, and land. Routine stuff, but at night everything was different. Judging closing speeds, altitudes, and distances was particularly difficult when the only reference points were those dancing wing lights and exhaust. Without a horizon, just keeping the plane straight and level was challenging. And since we didn't have radios, we had to watch for signal lamps and flares for course changes and landing instructions. The flight was an exercise in chaos, and I marveled that we all got down safely.

Then there were the precision landings, "shots to the circle," a technique that had to be mastered. The maneuver began by flying downwind toward a white chalk circle on a grass strip at an altitude of five hundred feet. Then when the circle was off my left wing I was instructed to throttle back to idle and begin my approach. The trick was to execute a 180-degree turn into the wind, at constant speed, in a gradual descent, timed precisely to make a three-point landing (wheels and tail touching down simultaneously) inside the circle—without touching the throttle.

Needless to say, it required plenty of practice—first with an instructor, and then solo. At first, I either soared helplessly over the circle, or grossly undershot it. But gradually, my ability to judge and adjust for changing wind directions and speeds throughout the turn improved and resulted in more and more successful landings. Confidence that I could hit at least two out of four on the "C-check," an absolute requirement to pass, was growing.

On 6 June 1944, black headlines announced that the long-awaited allied invasion of Europe was underway. I listened to recordings of General Eisenhower's radio announcement, read the sketchy reports, and continued to fly, buoyed by the news, and happily anticipating early victories. But with passing days, it became clear that the largest military operation in history was less than a resounding success. Casualty reports were sobering and unremitting. Battle lines were stagnant. It was weeks before the Allies broke through German defenses, and in a series of lightning thrusts, trapped tens of thousands of enemy soldiers, and demoralized most of the rest. Victory suddenly appeared in sight, and the possibility that the war might end before I graduated seeped uneasily into my consciousness.

Our flight training was in high gear. I was moving rapidly through the syllabus, flying every day but Sunday, building prowess and confidence. Progress was measured daily, and graded by check flights at the completion of each phase, designated by letters A through D. It was the ultimate pass-fail grading system: an arrow pointing up opposite the student's name on the scheduling blackboard and he passed; failure was an arrow pointing down. If the student received a "Down," he was required to get "Ups" on two consecutive check flights flown with different check pilots, or be washed out.

That had been standard procedure throughout navy flight training, and everyone understood it. However, a recent upsurge in the number of graduating pilots, together with lowered estimates of future need, had triggered a major reduction in the number of cadets in the training program. Standards were raised all across the board, and check pilots, in particular, were pressured to grade more stringently. Even worse, preflight schools like Chapel Hill, which I had just left, were now required to wash out the bottom half of each class en masse.

It was made crystal clear to us, verbally and in writing, that anyone harboring doubts about his ability or desire to complete the program should resign immediately, and those who stayed would be subject to immediate dismissal for any academic or disciplinary lapses. And if a cadet received a Down on a check flight, he was, in effect, washed out, for no one could fly two Ups in a row anymore. It became known throughout the navy as the "Purge."

A and B checks, early in the syllabus, were not very demanding, and almost every cadet passed. The C check, on the other hand, covered all the maneuvers, shots to circles, a simulated emergency landing, and every item in preflight inspection and ground procedures. Everything was on the line; the student's training, studying, hopes, and dreams—he would take off a cadet and could only hope to land as one. It was like taking an all-encompassing final exam, where the person giving and grading it was under heavy pressure to fail you.

Despite this, my confidence grew as the time for my C check approached. I discovered I was a good pilot, able to stand pressure, and (in practice anyway) could fly all the maneuvers with precision. But I also prepared meticulously for it. When flying solo, I always flew maneuvers in the sequence prescribed in check rides, practiced each to perfection before going on to the next, and constantly reminded myself to prepare for a simulated emergency landing. The day I was scheduled, I sat alone in a room for more than an hour, and thought through every aspect of the coming flight, from greeting the check pilot to the final landing. I mentally reviewed every detail of every maneuver—headings, speed, altitude, throttle setting, and contingency—with the intensity of an actual flight. When I finally walked out to meet the check pilot, I was ready.

Certain check pilots were noted for being more forgiving than other ones ("Santa Clauses," we called them), but the one I was assigned was not among them. The name chalked on the scheduling board for my flight was Lieutenant Hermalink, a serious, no-nonsense—appearing man of about thirty, whom I had never seen before. He arrived with his clipboard and parachute, I saluted (very crisply), and we walked out to the plane in silence. Preflight inspection, settling in our respective cockpits, and taxiing out continued without a word between us.

After takeoff, the flight proceeded in accordance with the planned syllabus. The mental run-through had cleared my mind to concentrate on the mechanics of a coordinated and smooth performance, and I knew the flight was going well, as he checked and graded each maneuver. I wound up the sequence by hitting two out of the first three shots to the circle, obviating a fourth shot, and was pulling up to head back to base when he cut the power. Emergency!

I looked around for a reasonably level pasture within gliding distance, calibrated my rate of descent, and planned the approach. Everything was proceeding beautifully. I would just clear a low stone wall, reach a grassy area, and have enough room to set the plane down and brake to a stop. Then, he suddenly pushed the throttle full forward, and said, "Okay, that's it, take me home. *You were landing downwind.*" I was stunned. I couldn't believe it. I had failed to check the wind direction! It meant an almost certain Down, and the end of my flying career. I was devastated.

As we flew back in silence, I reviewed my options. I could admit forgetting to check the wind direction, pledge never to do it again, plead for mercy, and hope for the best. Or I could ignore the lapse and focus on the fact that under the circumstances, the wind was really not strong enough to matter or affect the outcome. I was certain that if it had been an actual emergency, I would have made the selected field comfortably and landed safely. I chose the latter argument, realizing that I would be disputing the indisputable airman's dictum: "Never, never land downwind." And I would, at best, have only a couple of minutes to make my case.

We landed, and walked back to the hangar in silence. Then he stopped and turned to me and intoned the dreaded words: "I'm going to have to give you a DOWN." I responded with all the quiet conviction I could muster, "Sir, I certainly understand that a downwind landing is against standard procedure, but in this instance I believed that the wind wasn't strong enough to outweigh the advantages of the field and the approach I chose." He said, "But there were other fields to choose from that would have permitted a normal upwind approach." I responded, with just a touch more firmness, "That's true, but I was sure I could make this one, and in fact, it would have been a successful dead stick landing."

He looked at me quietly for a moment, weighing my argument, obviously agonizing over the decision. I said no more; in effect, resting my case. After an eternity of perhaps ten seconds, he abruptly turned on his heel, walked to the scheduling blackboard, and picked up a piece of chalk. Opposite my name he drew a line down, and then—an upside-down V at the top of it. And without looking back, he walked away. It was an arrow pointing UP. I had passed!

In many ways, the rest of the syllabus was anticlimactic. The D flight check was little more than a final review of our piloting skills, plus a basic cross-country exercise that few if any cadets failed. Ground-school exams were largely behind us. But the attrition rate had been brutal: only eleven of the twenty-five cadets in my platoon survived. It had been a summer of broken dreams, for every morning washed-out cadets could be seen slowly filing on to buses, subdued by the oppressive aura of failure, and headed for the diminished horizons of enlisted status. There were no good-byes, and no plans made to keep in touch, even among the closest friends. They just left, and none of us had the heart or the courage to try to console them.

But for the survivors, the situation was just the opposite: relief mixed with joy, tempered by the challenges ahead. We were off to Pensacola, the major leagues, where the planes were faster, naval aviators were anointed, officers were commissioned, and those glorious wings of gold were pinned on. I could almost taste it.

If there were a Mecca in naval aviation, Pensacola would be it. Located in the Florida panhandle, it was the birthplace of flight by the navy, its first training command, and the laboratory for many of the innovations and tactical refinements in naval aviation through the years. Here, we would fly our first low-wing monoplanes, made of metal instead of fabric, and really learn to navigate, fly on instruments, fire machine guns, and drop bombs. And it was here we would choose or be chosen for our ultimate flight designation, and my dream of becoming a fighter pilot would be either realized or dashed.

I arrived with cadets from several other primary flight schools, and again, became part of another twenty-five-man platoon, confident that Grosse Isle had prepared me well for the training ahead. At that time, Pensacola Naval Air Station consisted of "Mainside," the original base and headquarters of the training command, with an airfield and seaplane facility, and five outlying auxiliary airfields, each with complete operational flight and living facilities, many of them recently constructed. Cadets were moved through different fields for specialized training in each phase of the flight syllabus, and in about nine months, if successful, would return to Mainside for commissioning exercises and official designation as a naval aviator. At the beginning of the war, cadets began and completed their training at Pensacola, and it had taken us more than a year just to get there.

"Basic Training" began at Allison Field in our first "modern" airplane, the SNV Vultee monoplane, dubbed the Vibrator. As its nickname implied, it was noisy, with a big, thundering radial engine, nonretractable landing gear, a glassed-in canopy, and—finally—two-way radios. And it did vibrate more than any plane I ever flew. After a few flights with an instructor to get checked out, it was all solo flying, with the instructor leading us in his own plane. We learned the basics of flying in formation, various flight patterns, and mild acrobatic maneuvers.

We were also learning radio procedure, and from time to time, someone (we never really knew who) would make nonsensical transmissions, to the vast irritation of instructors who were trying to inculcate the disciplines of brevity, clarity, and navy protocols into our communications souls. At any given time, a voice transmission might be heard imitating the Green Hornet or perhaps the Shadow from popular radio programs. I still remember with a chuckle the day a voice broke the silence with, "Who dat," which was promptly answered by another voice saying, "Who dat, say who dat." Then the first voice came back with, "Who dat, say who dat, when I say who dat," at which point an instructor came on the air with the gruff order to "knock it off," and warning: "If I find out who's doing the talking he will be grounded." Momentary silence. Then the second voice, softly, "Who dat?" Most of us were still teenagers, and we thought it was pretty funny. The instructors, no doubt, thought otherwise.

After six weeks, we moved to Whiting Field to begin an intensive instrument-flight training program to prepare for all-weather flying. It is difficult for nonpilots to understand how challenging it is to control an airplane in zero-visibility conditions. At the very least, they think one could tell if the plane were banking, diving, or climbing. The reality, however, is that without the aid of flight instruments there is no frame of reference, and complete disorientation occurs within seconds. Moreover, the pilot's senses, rather than helping, actually aggravate the situation, making it impossible for him to know if he is banking, flying level, upside down, or even spinning. The condition is called vertigo, and without appropriate training, it is usually fatal.

Ground school and the use of a simulator called a Link Trainer familiarized us with each of many instruments we relied on, their characteristics, and their limitations. But it was sitting in the backseat of a plane, under a hood blocking all view of the outside, that we learned the rudiments and disciplines of controlling flight solely on instruments, building competency and confidence. The basic flight instruments included an artificial horizon to show the relationship with the ground, a turn and bank indicator, and a rate-of-climb (or dive) indicator, and of course, altimeter, speedometer, and a compass.

In flight, these instrument readings were always moving, in different sequences, giving different messages. The challenge was to scan all of the instruments continuously, making corrections as indicated on each, but never fixating on any one of them. It wasn't easy under the best of circumstances, and was almost impossible when natural senses argued against the instruments. Landing a plane under minimum ceiling and visibility conditions, especially in turbulent weather, was truly surfing on the edge of oblivion—powerfully concentrating mind and emotions.

Like every other phase of training, however, what seemed impossible at first, gradually became doable and eventually routine. I learned to ignore my senses and commit myself, and in effect, my life, to a reality defined solely by mechanical instruments. Just to make sure I stayed that way, I was periodically subjected to "unusual attitudes," the ultimate test. While I sat under the hood, the instructor would put the plane through a series of disorienting turns, dives and rolls, and then, with a terse "You've got it," turn it over to me. The plane might be inverted, in a steep climb, a precipitous dive, or anything in between. I would have only seconds to scan the spinning instruments, determine the plane's attitude, and effect recovery.

Once the instrument syllabus was completed, I was qualified for both military and civilian instrument ratings, and it was time to move on to the final training phase before graduation. Where I would go depended on the aircraft and missions assigned, and the training required. The first cut was between lighter-than-air (blimps) or heavier-than-air (airplanes). If airplanes, it was multiengine (transports and seaplanes) or single engine (dive bombers, torpedo bombers, or fighters). Although the selection process probably began as soon as I arrived in Pensacola, its course was never clear. I liked to think that an individual's choice was important, but undoubtedly, flight performance, instructor input, personality, and psychological profiles were the major determining factors.

I made clear my desire to fly fighters in every way possible, especially in official psychological questionnaires, where I answered every question, written or verbal, with the presumed fighter qualifications in mind. In a none-too-subtle manner, I tried to convey a thirst for sole responsibility, a passionate desire to rely on my own abilities, and a consummate joy in solitary activities. I also tried to project these characteristics in everything I did, in the air and on the ground. It was easy because it was exactly how I felt, hopefully making it all the more convincing.

As the cadet assignments began—first to lighter-than-air, then multiengine— and my name wasn't among them, I breathed a huge sigh of relief. Then I saw my name listed for single-engine training at Barron Field (a.k.a. "Bloody Barron"), narrowing my eventual assignment to torpedo bombers, dive bombers, or fighters. I was still in the running.

Meanwhile, letters from home, always determinedly cheerful, turned anxious. My brother Lloyd hadn't been heard from since being shipped to Europe more than a month earlier. The massive surprise German counterattack in what became the "Battle of the Bulge" was in full force, with heavy casualties reported; and we feared the worst. Although it was the Christmas season, the national mood was anything but festive. We could only wait and hope. Weeks passed before the German offensive was turned back, and eventually a letter arrived from Lloyd, saying little more than that he was all right. As I savored the news, I thought of all the families still waiting for a similar letter, or worse, learning they would never receive one.

At Barron, I checked out in another new plane, the North American SNJ. It was faster, sleeker, and had retractable landing gear—and didn't vibrate. We embarked on an intense four-month program of aerial gunnery, dive bombing, fighter tactics, and cross-country navigation flights. Again, precision was required and graded in everything we did. Although ground school continued, flying was the overriding activity, and perfection the overarching goal.

For the first time, an airplane became an extension of my being as I dove, climbed, rolled, and spun without thinking. It was akin to a trained athlete weaving, dodging, or leaping instinctively in the heat of a game. Pure fun, for most of the pressure was off. I was confident that only a major mistake like landing wheels up or running out of fuel would wash me out. But still there was no word on fighter selection. Then, one glorious day, sealed envelopes were handed out. Mine had a single sheet saying my next duty station was NAS Green Cove Springs, Florida—a base for fighter pilots! It was the happy culmination of almost two years of training, and a lifetime of dreaming.

There was only one last phase to complete: preoperational training in the SBD, the famed Dauntless Dive Bomber. My first flight in this combat aircraft had to be solo because the navy did not build dual versions of operational aircraft. The Dauntless was heavier, more powerful, and much larger than any plane I had flown, and I soon realized why it had such a sterling war record. Stable and heavily armored, with dive brakes making possible a steep angle of attack without building excessive speed, its design provided more time on target and greater accuracy. This, plus the skill of aggressive pilots, had turned the tide at the Battle of Midway, sinking four Japanese carriers in a matter of minutes. It was the turning point of the Pacific War.

Finally, in late April, I returned to Pensacola's Mainside, with all ground and air requirements fulfilled. Although trained as navy cadets, we now had a choice of being commissioned in either the marine corps or the navy. Most of us had long since made up our minds. Certainly, I had, because I loved the sea second only to the air, and the combination was nirvana. Besides, flying off aircraft carriers would be more challenging than airfields, and of course, army pilots couldn't do it. Some of my friends were equally enamored with the corps, and chose the marines primarily to fly Corsairs, the fighter plane of choice. As it turned out, I was commissioned in the navy and assigned Corsairs—the best of all worlds.

The excitement and anticipation of graduation began to build. I was fitted for an officer's uniform, and issued personal aviation gear. It included everything from light coveralls, summer jacket, and a cloth helmet, to heavy fur-lined leather flight pants, jacket, helmet, and boots, electrically wired for winter. This time, the pièce de résistance was an outsized Hamiliton wrist chronometer, with intricate timing mechanisms and dials to match. Author Tom Wolf later described it as the defining signature of a "fighter jock" in his book *The Right Stuff*.

At long last, on a bright sunny morning, I donned a new starched white uniform with single gold-striped epaulets signifying the rank of ensign, and lined up with about forty other cadets. When my name was called, I marched (floated?) forward, squaring each corner along the way, to stand at attention before the commandant. After an exchange of salutes and a few words of congratulations, he presented my commission as an officer in the United States Navy, a certificate designating me naval aviator number P21467 in the long history of naval aviation, and pinned on a pair of gorgeous, glittering gold wings. Those shimmering dreams of my youth had turned into reality after completing what arguably was the finest flight training program ever devised. Sadly, less than a third of my original classmates were there to share it.

CHAPTER 5

FIGHTERS

Whencing the ceremony ended, we strolled to bachelor officers' quarters, returning our first salutes along the way from sailors vying for the traditional dollar from newly minted ensigns. Our gear had been moved to our new quarters during the ceremony, and now we could hardly wait to have lunch and a toast or two at the hallowed officers club to celebrate. The euphoria was short lived, however, for I was handed a message that my mother was trying to reach me and to please call right away. Thinking it might be to congratulate me, my heart sank when I heard her say in a soft but steady voice, "Dad is very sick. I'm not sure he's going to make it, you should come home right away."

I immediately departed on emergency leave on a somber flight to Boston, where my father was recovering from a major operation. I had been shielded from knowing the seriousness of his illness—bladder cancer—until after the commissioning ceremony. When I entered his room at the Deaconess Hospital, I was stunned by the physical devastation the disease had caused. A robust man, weighing more than 180 pounds, had been reduced to a cadaverous one hundred pounds. I hardly recognized him.

My mother and sister had rented a small apartment nearby, and were spending most of their waking hours by his side, talking to and encouraging him. I liked to think that my presence also helped a little, but there was no real improvement by the time my emergency leave ended and I had to go. It took several months—one in the hospital and the rest in that little apartment—before he recovered enough to travel home. A skilled surgeon and the loving care of my mother and sister had saved his life against heavy odds.

I returned to Florida and operational training at Green Cove Springs, a small naval air station near Jacksonville. I had been slated to fly the gull-winged Corsair, my first choice, but lost my place while on emergency leave, and was assigned the F4F Grumman Wildcat instead. Although not as fast or as maneuverable as the Japanese Zero, this carrier-based fighter had played a critical role in the early part of the war, with its greater firepower (six fifty-caliber machine guns), more armor protection, and demonstratively superior pilot training.

Still, I was disappointed, for the Wildcat was hardly state-of-the-art from the pilot's point of view. Instead of being hydraulically operated, twenty-eight and a half strenuous turns of a hand crank were required to raise and lower the landing gear, a smaller crank to adjust cowl flaps, and two men on the ground to fold and spread its wings. Merely hitting a switch in newer navy fighters accomplished the same things.

Now officially designated naval aviators, we no longer had to defer to instructors, or worry about getting washed out. Learning became more of a cooperative enterprise—a marvelous release from almost two years of tension. We were split into divisions of five, and assigned an instructor with recent combat experience. Ours was a soft-spoken full lieutenant just back from fleet duty, with several enemy planes to his credit. Although in his early twenties, he seemed much older and more than a little bored by instructor duty. Nevertheless, he was a good teacher, and worked hard to mold us into professional fighter pilots by example as well as word—and by insisting on a disciplined, coordinated approach to everything we did.

He flew on most flights, briefing us before take off, leading, demonstrating, and commenting as we went through our paces, then critiquing again upon landing. Rather than rotating his wing man as most instructors did, he permanently appointed me early on without comment. At first, I wondered if he thought I needed extra help, but soon was happy to learn he just felt more comfortable with me on his wing. Beyond the obvious vote of confidence, I was given a unique opportunity to gain close-in experience with a true professional.

We flew mornings and afternoons and occasionally at night, running through the usual rolls, loops, and tactical maneuvers. We tightened up formation flying, streamlined radio procedures, and flew as if in combat, always aware of our position, and constantly looking for other planes in the sky. We developed greater accuracy in dive bombing and strafing, and were introduced to a variety of intricate aerial gunnery runs designed to attack enemy planes while limiting exposure to return fire. Our runs were made on a long banner-like "sleeve" towed by one of us, rotated daily. Coming in at high speeds and varying angles required skill and a great deal of practice to get into position to aim, fire, and recover after flashing by.

Bullets from each pilot's six machine guns were daubed with a different colored paint-like substance to identify and attribute holes in the target upon return. The banner went unscathed at first as we struggled to adjust to rapidly changing distances, speeds, and angles for that split-second burst of fire. Before long, however, we gathered around the banner to find it riddled with holes; mercifully, some were mine.

Dogfighting, I learned, was essentially a gigantic game of chicken. We practiced tactics and techniques, building up tolerance for the brutal gravity forces bearing down on our bodies. I learned and applied such fighter-pilot dictums as keep your head on a swivel, protect your tail, and always, always turn inside the enemy if you hope to survive. Most fights devolved into a series of scissorlike turns, with each pilot pulling as many "Gs" as he could stand, trying to get "inside" the other, while flying on the edge of a high-speed stall. Too many Gs and you black out; stall, and you lose control of your plane, and the enemy winds up on your tail. Either way, you're dead.

We paired up and practiced among ourselves, and then one at a time against the instructor. He usually, but not always, won by winding up on the student's tail, in position to shoot him down. In debriefings, he dissected each student's mistakes, explaining what should have been done. If one of us happened to win, he would explain why, and managed to seem almost as pleased as the winner at the victory.

We practiced various defensive tactics, the most famous being the "Thatch Weave" developed by Jimmy Thatch, a celebrated fighter pilot in the Pacific. The Weave was particularly useful when defending slower bombers against superior enemy numbers. It was simplicity itself. The fighter escort, as usual, flew above the bombers, and if attacked, went into a high-speed weave, crossing head-on, with his wingman at each pass ready to protect his tail from enemy fire. These and other tactics were constantly evolving from combat and quickly adopted in operational training, improving the navy's kill rate as the war progressed.

In three months, I was a professional navy fighter pilot, flying without thinking, bombing, strafing, attacking, and defending with precision and consummate confidence—except I had yet to land on a carrier. Qualification to operate on carriers was a carefully prescribed program developed over many years, at the cost of many lives. It set forth flight patterns, protocols, and intricate coordinated responsibilities between ship crews and flight personnel. The number, quality, and frequency of carrier landings for each pilot were specified and monitored to maintain certification. Success in carrier qualification and you were one of a small band of elite aviators; failure, and you might be dead, although few of us thought of it in those terms.

Training procedures began by unlearning that hoary tenant of safe flight: "You may fly low or slow, but never, ever fly low *and* slow." The carrier-landing pattern, by necessity, had to be flown at very low altitudes, and only a few knots above stalling speed, leaving little room to recover from any miscalculation. Added to this is the challenge of flying a tight turning approach to land on a small section of a deck that is likely to be bobbing and rolling in the ocean's waves. All this while responding to a landing signal officer perched at the end of that deck, waving brightly colored paddles as you approach.

A miraculous symbiotic relationship soon develops between LSO and pilot, as the LSO conveys through paddle movements that the pilot is "too slow," "too fast," "too high," or "too low." The pass culminates when the plane is "in the groove" (just before reaching the deck), and the LSO must signal either a "wave off" to go around if the pass is unsatisfactory, or a "cut" to land. These latter commands are mandatory, requiring immediate full power or none regardless of the pilot's judgment. All other signals during the approach are discretionary.

Field carrier landing practice is the first phase, conducted on a runway painted with lines to simulate a flight deck. The LSO and his assistant are stationed on the left edge of the "deck" when viewed from the plane. As the pilot makes a tight turn at treetop level on final approach, he is picked up by the LSO, who begins "waving" him in. Running comments on each pass is dictated to the assistant by the LSO to review with the pilot at the end of the day. I soon became sufficiently comfortable and received enough passing grades to move from carrier landing practice to the real thing.

Early the next morning, I packed flight gear and enough clothes for a week and climbed into a bus carrying fifteen other pilots and headed for Mayport, a harbor near Jacksonville. There we boarded a small navy launch and put out to sea to rendezvous with the carrier USS *Salomon Seas*. The weather was windy and cloudy; and the sea was breaking over the bow, drenching us even at moderate speeds. Although uncomfortable, this was the combination of flying and boating that originally attracted me to naval aviation, and I was so excited I could hardly stand it—a sentiment not widely shared by the other pilots.

As we pulled alongside the carrier, a major challenge awaited—timing the jump from the launch to the carrier boarding platform while each was bobbing wildly in different sequences. The old navy hands enjoyed watching supposedly intrepid aviators digging deep for the courage to make the leap.

After jumping onboard, I stowed my gear and went topside to look around. This ship was one of the famous jeep carriers, so named for their relatively small size and flimsy construction. They had originally been designed as merchant ships and hastily converted to small "escort" aircraft carriers to help compensate for the dire shortage of carriers after Pearl Harbor. Their primary mission was escorting supply ships, but too often they became engaged in deadly sea battles in the Pacific. Their hulls were so thin that when a wave got out of sync with the ship's motion, reverberations like a blow against an oil drum coursed through the ship, followed inevitably by a loud boom when the panels sprung back. Wry humor had it that a jeep carrier could take two torpedoes: one through it and the other over.

A friend and I were standing on the windy flight deck, trying to steady ourselves while marveling at the fore and aft pitching and rocking in the heavy seas. Somewhat in awe, I said, "Can you imagine trying to land on this thing on a day like this?" Before he could respond, a loudspeaker erupted with the order, repeated several times, "PILOTS, REPORT TO THE READY ROOM IMMEDIATELY TO PREPARE FOR FLIGHT OPERATIONS." In no time, we were suited up, briefed, and in our planes, preparing to take off in these "unimaginable" conditions.

I seldom doubted my ability to do anything other similarly endowed people could do, but this would surely test that view. Just taxiing the Wildcat was daunting because its narrow landing gear and extraordinarily soft oleo struts allowed it to rock steeply with the rolling ship. When parked or taxiing near the edge of the deck, tipping over into the roiling sea seemed a distinct possibility. There was no time to dwell on that unhappy thought, however, as I found myself in line for takeoff. When my turn came, the launching officer signaled to set brakes, rev engine to full power, check instruments, and on his signal release brakes. I was airborne almost before I knew it. With some thirty knots of wind over the deck (actual wind plus ship speed), only an additional fifty or so knots generated by my engine were necessary to reach flying speed.

As instructed, I picked up the appropriate interval with the plane ahead, entered the landing pattern, and started my approach: a 180-degree turn to hit an imaginary spot on the flight deck with my tail hook. Not unlike those "shots to the circle" I worked so hard to master in primary, except this "circle" was moving, pitching, and rolling. Because of slow flight, I had to hold the plane's nose high and the engine cowl flaps wide open, obscuring my view of the flight deck.

The LSO was left suspended on his tiny platform, seemingly hanging over the water, to guide me in. Trying to manipulate the controls, adjust the throttle, and hold the plane a few knots above stalling was like walking a tightrope on a windy day, as I maneuvered in the groove. Inevitably, my first pass resulted in a wave off. On the second one, somewhat to my surprise, I received a cut, snapped back the throttle, pushed the nose forward, saw the pitching and rolling deck for the first time, and just before slamming down, eased the stick back to land. Almost simultaneously, my body strained against the safety straps as the plane abruptly stopped and rolled slowly backward. I had caught a wire. I was a carrier pilot. I was proud—and I was vastly relieved.

Over the next two days, we worked on various formations and breakups used in carrier operations, and practiced landings and takeoffs until we had the required minimum of eight satisfactory landings for certification as carrier qualified. I gradually became more comfortable, but never complacent coming aboard. Taxiing, on the other hand, remained daunting.

We returned to Green Cove Springs to wind up operations, and prepare for assignment to the fleet for combat duty. We expected to be formed into five-pilot combat teams and inserted into active squadrons. But because I had volunteered for night-fighter duty (more challenging), I was slated for a few additional weeks of training on the West Coast in the more advanced Grumman F6F, which was equipped with the latest instrumentation and still highly secret radar. But suddenly the world changed, and all of our training, studying, worrying, and hard work were rendered unessential. An American bomber named *Enola Gay* had dropped the first atomic bomb on Hiroshima, Japan.

As the devastating results came in, it was clear the war would soon be over. The actual surrender occurred a few days later after another bomb was dropped on Nagasaki. I celebrated VJ day in downtown Jacksonville in a day and night of unrestrained joy and unspoken thanksgiving, to say nothing about national pride. The entire nation was caught up in a spontaneous, uninhibited celebration that, in many ways, was the perfect bookend to the shock of Pearl Harbor a few tragic years earlier.

Of course everything changed. We had spent years preparing for a contest that had been called off at the last minute and (we thought) would never to be rescheduled. Despite all of the celebrating, I confess to feeling a little let down. It was like waiting to take the field for a football game, and having it summarily canceled—relieved that I hadn't been injured or lost the game, but disappointed that I hadn't had a chance compete.

Instead of joining the fleet for the final battle against Japan, I was ordered to Brown Field just outside of San Diego to help downsize and rearrange equipment and facilities. Most of my time was spent ferrying aircraft to bases designated for storage or salvage. The most heavily traveled route was from the West Coast to Clinton, Oklahoma, where a huge field was used to park aircraft of every description for mothballing or salvage. Too often, I flew the two-day route in shiny new fighter planes, parked, climbed out, and left them never to be flown again.

As my separation from the service approached, I was transferred to North Island Naval Air Station near San Diego, where I flirted briefly with the thought of making a career in the navy. I loved flying, a naval officer's life was comfortable, and my financial future would be secure, but I quickly decided that military life during peacetime was not for me. I would have too little control over my life.

My only moment of doubt occurred as I emerged from the naval air station's headquarters building, where I had started the process for release from active duty. I heard a loud roar overhead and looked up to see a strange aircraft go streaking by. It had the conventional propeller in its nose, but also what appeared to be a jet engine in its tail section. I learned it was an experimental plane built by Ryan Aviation, called the Fire Ball, one of the first U.S. jets to undergo flight tests. I was at once impressed and saddened as I realized the navy would soon have operational jets, and I would never fly one. The next morning, I boarded a navy transport plane and flew back to New England and civilian life—as a passenger.

CHAPTER 6

HOMECOMING

Returning home after years of military service was a complex, emotional experience; heartwarming, of course, yet unsettling. It was a time to turn on the lights, celebrate victory, and return to normalcy. But it was also a time to recognize, confront, and adjust to change. I will never forget the pleasure and excitement of reuniting with my family. The loving hug and unrestrained joy of my mother as my beaming father waited his turn, then his brief handshake that turned into a bear hug—the first since I was a little boy. They, who had labored so hard, so successfully, to hide their worry during those long years, were granted their own private peace.

Then I joined the happy hugging and backslapping greetings of old girlfriends and buddies. We were all anxious to catch up with the past, and everyone talked at once. But in the midst of those joyful reunions crept a palpable feeling of unease as I slid back into a mundane world, one without overarching cause or expanding horizons. Every person and every relationship had changed, of course. Fond, old memories were overtaken and often supplanted by tales of wartime experiences, complicating and sometimes forestalling renewed friendships. In short, the veteran had changed; the girl back home had not. And, regrettably, while we were immersed in our own reentry to civilian life, little time was spent thinking of those who would never return, and the silent pain endured by their families as the homecoming celebrations rolled on.

Swapping stories, often over cold beers, with other vets was great fun. Only the good times were recounted, and few if any of the terrible aspects of war were acknowledged. Whether this was an effort to forget, deny, or simply avoid difficult memories, or simply a desire to accentuate the positive, it was universal. An uninvolved observer might easily conclude that World War II was a lark, and that reports of killed, maimed, and missing were more apocryphal than real. Yet in almost every bull session of any size, anywhere in the country, there were veterans who had engaged in brutal combat too terrible to recount and impossible to forget. My older brother Lloyd, for example, had been in the Battle of the Bulge, where casualties and atrocities were horrendous, and yet he only spoke of peripheral aspects of the experience: the bitter cold, forced marches, and the drudgery of digging and sleeping in foxholes in frozen ground. And even those stories were told with a humorous twist where possible.

And then, of course, the official homecoming celebration: the inevitable parade with its array of uniforms, relaxed marching, high-school bands, a drum corps, and wailing fire trucks and police cars, all flanked by the "home front," cheering and waving flags, and ending up at the baseball field for speeches by "dignitaries." Everyone seemed excited but the vets, yet most joined in. I had other ideas.

Securing sponsorship by a local businessman, I organized a mini-air show: with two former army pilots and me flying Piper Cubs. My idea was to perform aerobatics over the parade, and end with dramatic low-level passes over the crowded baseball field. Flying in loose formation, we did a series of wingovers and chandelles, climaxing with (almost) simultaneous tailspins, all of which (we were told later) were interesting but not inspiring ("too far away"). The low-level passes, on the other hand, got more attention—much more—for unfortunately they coincided with a series of passionate orations by dignitaries, to their discomfort and the crowd's amusement. The businessman elected not to publicize his involvement in the airshow; we enjoyed a mixed reception at the

"Homecoming Ball" that evening, dancing in the town square and in the National Guard Armory. I still thought it was better than marching.

I continued to fly from time to time, taking buddies and girlfriends up for sightseeing (or show boating) rides, and for the brave, heart-stopping aerobatics. One bright summer weekend, I casually asked my mom and dad if they would like to go for an airplane ride, knowing full well that they had never been up in an airplane. After some discussion, they agreed to drive to the airport, but deferred the decision of actually going up. We talked along the way about the possible flight, what it would be like, and what we would see, and after a while my dad averred "it might be all right." He was strapped into the front seat, sat straight up, and gripped the supporting rods on either side of the windshield for takeoff. He continued to look straight ahead as we climbed, still holding on to the rods, and managed to stay vertical to the ground by leaning right when I entered a mild turn to the left. Then I banked right, and he leaned left. I ever so gradually steepened the turns, and watched with amusement as he tried to counteract them. When it was no longer possible, he settled into his seat, looking straight ahead, those rods still firmly clasped just in case. After a short ride over Berlin, pointing out our home and commenting on how small people and cars looked, I landed and taxied back to the line.

His confidence restored, he pronounced the flight "all right" and encouraged my mother to go up. She was more relaxed and quiet, and busily looked around as I climbed. I was beginning to think she was enjoying the flight, when she said, "Chobe, how high are we now?" "A little over eleven hundred feet," I replied. "That's high enough," she said firmly. Back home, they were quite pleased with themselves, and I enjoyed their matter-of-fact description of the experience to their friends, but to my knowledge, they never flew in an airplane again.

All too soon, the need to pick up the pieces of civilian life began to intrude on the homecoming scene. Decisions had to be made whether to resume college or get a job, and for several of my friends, when to marry the girl-back-home. I, like most, was anxious to get going again and couldn't wait to return to the

University of New Hampshire. I found I could be reinstated for the second semester beginning in a few weeks, and jumped at the chance. A happy surprise was the GI Bill, a new and farsighted program paying full tuition plus seventy-five dollars a month for veterans engaged in recognized educational pursuits. I still got a job while in college, but the need was far less dire than before.

For those deciding to work instead of going to school, the government paid twenty dollars a week for one year while they were looking for a job. The program was immediately dubbed the Fifty-Two-Twenty Club. In order to join and maintain membership, a veteran had to provide a list of jobs for which he was qualified to his local government employment office; and if one were offered, he had to take it. I was surprised to see so many of my friends still out of work some six months later, busily "commiserating" together at the local tavern. I asked one of them, "How come? There seems to be plenty of jobs around." With a happy grin he replied, "Not for tail gunners!"

Returning to college in Durham was nostalgic and surreal. The campus itself was essentially unchanged, but the student body had been replaced with strangers. Most of the students I knew in 1943 had dropped out, graduated, or were veterans yet to return. Those who had enrolled, in the meantime, seemed uncommonly young, inexperienced, and predominately female. Class work was also vastly different. The subject matter was, of course, deeper and more intellectually demanding than the "how to" of intense military training; and the pace and scheduling was almost glacial in comparison. But there was a seriousness among students, especially veterans, that was markedly different from prewar days. Most of us were in a hurry to make up for lost time, and no longer thought in terms of four discrete years of college, punctuated by long summer vacations. At least, I didn't. Less than a month after leaving active duty, I was back in Durham loading up credit hours to the maximum, and planning to continue through summer school. After all, I was twenty-two years old, and feeling the mighty weight of passing time.

But it was also fun. Fraternity life resumed, athletic teams were reestablished, and we had learned a thing or two about partying. There were, however, major adjustments to be made in the dating game. "Girls" had to be in their dorms or sororities by 10:00 p.m., and written permission was needed to stay out all night or be away on weekends. Sorority parties were under the watchful eye of an ever-present housemother and consisted of light refreshments (nonalcoholic), dancing (not too close), and at ten o'clock sharp, the inevitable joining of hands in a circle to sing the sorority song with the lights turned down low. Whatever romanticism this engendered was quickly shattered when the lights were snapped on, and the housemother ushered us out the door.

Fraternity parties, on the other hand, were something else because we were in control. Many of the same rules applied, of course, but were followed considerably less stringently. Instead of a housemother, we recruited known liberal-thinking chaperones from among the faculty. Alcohol, forbidden in any form, mysteriously appeared in many ordinary soft drinks. And when the lights were low, who knew what occurred in the nooks and alcoves of the floor above, to which no one was supposed to stray. All pretty tame stuff, but we learned to abide by, bend, and occasionally break the rules as the occasion arose—all the while taking a certain comfort from having them in place. Small wonder my generation had such difficulty adjusting to the coed dorms and freedom accorded our sons and daughters when they entered college.

Underlying all the adjusting and accommodations to civilian life was the imperative of planning the future, and the immediate need to select a major and sign up for the required courses. When a freshman, I had leaned toward a medical career but now, three years later, the extended training before starting a practice seemed far too long. But I was still drawn to the independence afforded by a profession, and the thought of getting a job and working for someone else for the rest of my life remained chilling. Among professions considered, dentistry was out, optometry was possible, and law and investment banking were not even on the screen, for I knew so little about them. In the end, I selected a major on the basis of credits in hand, courses available, and credits needed to graduate—as soon as possible—and deferred the decision of what to do then. I majored in psychology.

A few of the courses taken while in the navy qualified for credits, and I added the minimum number required for my major. Then I signed up for the maximum allowed in a well-rounded liberal arts curriculum on through summer school and the following year. I worked just hard enough to be on the dean's list and (I thought) to graduate cum laude. I consistently made the dean's list, but outsmarted myself on cum laude. I just missed the overall grade-point average required by getting a C+ in a boring seminar course, in which I felt certain of a B from test scores. "Lack of enthusiasm and poor class participation were the reasons for the lower grade," the professor gravely informed me, and I couldn't deny it. I graduated in June 1947.

More by the process of elimination than enthusiastic career selection, I applied to the Northern Illinois College of Optometry in Chicago, and was accepted for the following winter semester. I found the early courses in biological sciences interesting enough, but never particularly challenging. I began by earning high honors, and gradually slipped to average grades as the curriculum moved on to refraction, prescriptions, and fitting eyeglasses, and my interest waned. Working with patients in the clinical phase rekindled some attraction, but by the time I graduated in June 1950, I had serious doubts about optometry as a career. But once again, fate intervened, and the course of my life changed.

I had joined a naval reserve fighter squadron, VF-721, at the Glenview Naval Air Station some twenty-five miles north of downtown Chicago. In many ways, it was the saving grace of my time in the city, and probably the principal reason for staying in school. It required one weekend of training each month, plus an intense two-week training "cruise," generally land-based but occasionally at sea, each year. I signed up in January 1949, shortly before the squadron was scheduled to fly to Pensacola, to requalify for carrier operations.

It was like a breath of fresh air, and I was determined to go, but I would have to get checked out, quickly, in a plane I had never flown—the Grumman F6F Hellcat, bigger, more powerful, and much more advanced than the F4F. After a four-year lay off, carrier qualifications would be daunting, and I only had time for a few touch-and-go landings and an hour or so in general flight before taking off for Pensacola (still Mecca) and the carrier.

Upon arrival, the squadron set up operations at an outlying field, and we began field carrier landings. With so few hours in the Hellcat, I was clearly "pushing it," thinking instead of just doing, a dangerous-condition when flying low-and-slow patterns required for carrier operations. On the second pass, I got a little too slow in the groove. The plane started to loose flying speed, the controls got mushy, and I was on the verge of stalling—at that altitude, certain to be fatal. To regain flying speed, I reacted normally by thrusting the throttle forward expecting a burst of power, but instead, the handle came off in my hand!

Without additional power, I lost aileron control, my left wing dropped, my nose started down, and the plane swerved to the left. I saw the LSO and his assistant, almost in slow motion, drop paddles and notebook, and run for cover. And in that split second, I clearly envisioned the likely crash sequence. My left wing would hit the runway first, causing the plane to cartwheel, crushing the right wing as the plane smashed into the concrete and exploded in a fiery crash. Dispassionately, I even calculated my chances of survival, concluding they were not good. That filmy vision lives in my mind today, just as clear and bright, and still in slow motion.

Instinct alone prompted me to jam full right rudder to skid the plane to the right, providing just enough extra lift to the left wing for it to clear the runway as my wheels slammed down on the runway. I bounced high, cushioned the second landing with what little control I had left, and braked frantically as I fumbled for the short stub of the throttle to reduce power and finally come to a stop. I sat there for a moment to compose myself and deal with the reality that any other action on my part and the sirens would be wailing, and I would be history.

I grasped the stub on the throttle linkage, and managed to extract enough power to taxi slowly to the hangar area, feeling more and more relieved and rather proud that I was handling the incident so coolly. But as I raised my feet above the rudder pedals to maintain braking power, a traumatic quiver from the close call permeated my being and my knees began to shake uncontrollably. Try as I might, I couldn't stop them until safely back in the chocks. I had never experienced anything like that before or ever again despite similar close calls.

When the ground crew came out to greet me, crowding around to find out what happened, I held up the handle, and let them know with feeling that someone had failed to maintain the plane properly, or more precisely, "had screwed up." Although I could be faulted for getting slow in the groove, it would have been no big deal with power to correct it. And it bothered me to think that if I had crashed and not survived, the throttle failure would have likely gone undiscovered, and the accident would have been ruled "100 percent pilot error." Not an enviable epitaph; I was happy to be around to testify to the contrary.

Subsequent field carrier landings went well, and we were soon lifted aboard the USS *Cabot*, a midsized independence-class carrier, and put to sea. It was exciting to be aboard a navy ship again, especially after the years of mundane civilian life, and it was surprising how quickly the squadron got back up to speed. We all regained our carrier qualifications without incident, and over the next week, flew an intensive, carefully planned schedule of gunnery, bombing, and strafing hops, polishing old techniques and developing new ones. Operations were suspended over the weekend for a two-day visit to Havana.

Those were pre-Castro days, and the city was wide open. One of the squadron's senior officers rented a suite of rooms at the plush Hotel Nacional that immediately became the pilots' unofficial headquarters for nonstop partying and a few cursory visits to historical sites. Then it was back to the ship, hangovers and all, to pick up the training regimen. It was hard to believe we were actually being paid to have so much fun, but as events would prove, the navy and American taxpayers would get their money's worth in Korea.

Back in Chicago, squadron activities were intertwined with routine school life, leavening the ordinary with adventure. One such activity was the opening and dedication of O'Hare International Airport. Chicago had outgrown Midway Airport which was too embedded in suburbia to expand. An underused air force base about twenty miles north of Chicago was selected for decommissioning and transfer to the city to create an international airport, leaving Midway to service more local traffic. Ironically, this former air force field was then named for a navy pilot, Edward "Butch" O'Hare, who had grown up in Chicago and lost his life in World War II. He was one of the first night fighters in the navy, a small band of aviators flying F6Fs trained to use newly developed radar to protect the carrier after dark. It was the duty I had volunteered for and was scheduled to begin just before the war ended.

At 1646, on February 20, 1942, Butch O'Hare was launched from the carrier USS *Lexington* and returned to the darkened deck two hours later an ace. Incredibly, he had found and shot down five approaching enemy aircraft using a small blurry radarscope less than eight inches in diameter. Although instantly renowned in the fleet and acclaimed a hero in the United States, he had little time to enjoy his fame, for a few weeks later he took off on a similar night mission and never returned. He was awarded the Congressional Medal of Honor posthumously. It was fitting that Chicago's new airport be named O'Hare; it was unusual that the navy, not the air force, would put on an air show for the dedication. We could hardly wait.

The show began with a mass flyover by nearby navy squadrons flying various single-engine planes. We had recently replaced our F6F Hellcats with F8F Grumman Bearcats, reputed to be the fastest propeller-driven airplane ever built, and four of us were invited to show it off in a series of maneuvers and low-level passes. I thought it important to really learn to fly the plane in preparation for the show, and went out to Glenview on my own time to do it. The plane was "all engine," with a small cockpit, a seat practically resting on the floor, and a short control stick rising between the pilot's outstretched legs. Highly maneuverable, it could approach the speed of sound under its own power and potentially exceed it in a dive. However, no airplane had yet been designed to "break the sound barrier." Several attempts had resulted in disaster.

I decided to see how the plane handled when approaching the speed of sound, partly out of curiosity but mostly to recognize and avoid getting into a dangerous situation. Flying at about fifteen thousand feet, I moved the throttle to full power and pushed over into a shallow dive. As my speed increased, the F8F began buffeting mildly with a flutteringlike sound from the buildup of shock waves on its wing surfaces. I held the stick forward, watching my airspeed build, until the plane felt like a car running faster and faster over a rutted dirt road. The flutter had turned into violent buffeting, causing the controls to vibrate wildly, and emitting a low roar that I could hear in the cockpit.

There was still one more test: I pushed the nose down a little farther, easing closer to six hundred knots, and the plane started to "tuck under" despite pulling back on the stick—just as the manuals warned. I was within seconds of losing control and risking a fatal breakup. I reduced throttle, pulled my nose back to level flight, and let my pulse rate return to normal. I was satisfied that the danger was real and recognizable. "Going too fast" had now joined "going too slow" in fighter tactics—a hazard to be avoided on pain of death. Other than that, the F8F Bearcat was a dream to fly.

The giant flyover with different aircraft models from a number of airfields in the area was the opening event of the show. Joining up with them and forming a reasonably tight formation was in itself challenging. Formation flying, regardless of the number of planes involved, requires each pilot to maintain his position on the plane off his wing, and in turn, will have another pilot flying off him. Consequently, a small throttle change by the leader of a large formation will be progressively magnified down the line, and require major changes at the tail end. Similarly, planes on the outside of a turn have to speed up just to stay in place, not unlike the end of a "whip" when ice skaters join hands in a line. After almost an hour of trying to get everyone in position, we were approaching the field when one of the leader's tanks ran dry.

He immediately switched to another one, but it was too late to avoid a brief loss of power, causing everyone in the formation to overrun his position despite quickly snapping his own throttle back. It was not an auspicious beginning for the show. Adding to the disarray and almost prompting disaster was the leader's failure to maintain sufficient altitude for each plane to step down behind the next. Flying on the outer fringe, I was stepped down far below the leaders of the formation as we passed over downtown Chicago. Out of the corner of my eye, I saw the tip of an antenna on the top of one of the highest buildings slip by—just a few feet below my right wing. Had I been any lower, the air show and dedication could have ended before it began, and I would have been part of its history.

Fortunately, from then on everything went smoothly. After the flyover, the formation broke up into small units to perform a variety of maneuvers to entertain the crowd. The next-to-the-last event was our demonstration of the operational capabilities of the F8F. As part of that four-plane division, I was scheduled to fly simulated fighter tactics and dive-bombing runs leading up to a mock strafing attack, firing blanks from my six machine guns at low altitude. "Not low enough and too far from the crowd," radioed the controller in charge of the show after the first pass. He must not have known how fighter pilots would react. It was all we needed. The next run parted the crowd as we streaked by with only a few feet to spare. That and twenty-four machine guns firing at point-blank range certainly impressed the crowd, and might well have been the highlight of the show, except the famed Blue Angels were next.

Theirs was truly the grand finale, a spectacular signature performance of this six-plane team. Organized only a few years earlier in 1946, they were already a legend, although I had never seen them perform. The Blue Angels flew closer, faster, and with greater precision than any team before them. Their purpose was to demonstrate the equipment and skills of navy fighter pilots, to build public support for the navy's recruiting programs. As they frequently made clear, all naval aviators could fly the same maneuvers as they, though not with quite the same precision, and certainly not as close to the ground.

At a reception after the air show, I chatted briefly with several of them and was fascinated to hear how they happened to join the Blue Angels, how often they practiced, the signals they used, and disciplines they followed to make it all work. One rule I particularly remember was that all of them, married or single, dined together and retired at the same time the night before each performance to ensure that everyone was well rested for the next day's show. They were an impressive group in their gray flannels and blue blazers sporting a Blue Angel breast patch filigreed in gold. I envied them.

Without doubt, the training and friendships gained from serving with VF-721 were the highlights of my stay in Chicago, and provided a pleasant contrast to my otherwise ordinary life as a student, but it was all about to come to an end. As June 1950 and graduation day rolled around, I spent what I thought was my last weekend drill at Glenview and said my farewells. I was saddened to leave the squadron but otherwise happy to have finally finished school and received the doctor of optometry degree. I packed up, said good-bye to classmates, and headed back to Berlin. As always, there was a certain melancholy mixed with anticipation in the overall leave-taking, and I doubted I would see many of them again. But however dubious I was about optometry as a career, it was time to go to work at last; and I was looking forward to it. It was then that fate intervened, big time, halfway around the world.

Grandparents I never knew

Mother and Dad, newly married about 1910

Mother with my wings, 1945

My father, about 1940

Ten years old

Boyhood home

Berlin High School, 1942

On leave from flight school, 1943

Butch and I together—in Berlin, 1944

With Gerry visiting from war production work in
Hartford, & Stan home on furlough from Army, 1944

Lloyd home before going overseas

World War II propeller plane

It's cold up there

A carrier-qualified fighter pilot

Between wars—graduating from University of New Hampshire, 1947

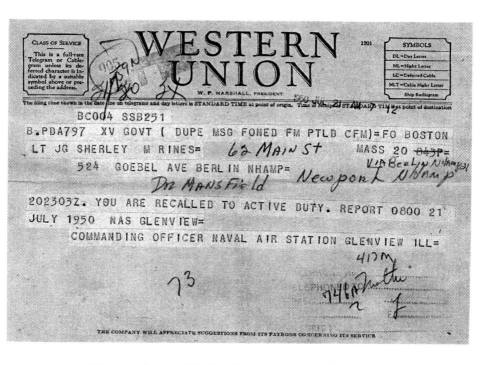

Korea explodes—VF-721 first reserve squadron called

Greetings at Naval Air Station North Island, Cal 1950

We get brand new jets

After hours

Division 5—"Mello" Rines, "Charley" Leary, "Whitey" Lichtfuss, "Jimbo" Dodge.

Training on Land

And at sea

USS Boxer, combat ready

Attaching bridle to catapult

Launch!

Airborne

Fast, in the groove

Cut!

Catching a wire

Missed approach—pilot survived

Refueling

Destroyer escort along side for refueling

We hit them

They hit us

45,000th landing aboard Boxer—the Captain

The Landing Signal Officer

Homecoming, October 1951

Mona Freeman on Hollywood set—
with squadron mate Joe Quirk

Terry Moore

Mary Jo Marcy

Uncle Arthur

Marcy, Jeff, David, &Tosca, about 1968

Jeffrey William Rines
1957-1978

Skiing the Headwall with Marcy and Jeff, about 1976

Mary Jo Rines—Artist

Part 3

KOREA

On June 25, 1950, just five years after the end of WW II, the North Korean Army swarmed over the Thirty-eighth Parallel into South Korea. Within days, President Truman committed aircraft, and then American troops in defense of South Korea, but in numbers too small and equipment too limited to stem the tide. Pushed into a small perimeter, they held until more U.S. troops arrived under the UN banner and regained the initiative. A series of seesaw battles extending from the Yalu River in the North (where hordes of Chinese "volunteers" attacked) and the Thirty-eighth Parallel, where it all began, continued until an uncertain ceasefire was negotiated in 1953.

I was recalled in July 1950, without warning, to learn to fly and fight in jets, the culmination of years of training to be a fighter pilot. The following chapters describe fifty-five combat missions over Korea and flight-instruction duty upon my return. Then it was back to civilian life again, marriage, and the beginning of a new career.

CHAPTER 7

"YOU ARE RECALLED TO ACTIVE DUTY"

I arrived home to prepare for my new career. There were state board exams to study for and decisions to make about when and where to open a practice and how to finance it. And although I had no plans to stay in Berlin, I had many friends and relationships to renew. All this came to a sudden end on the morning of July 24, 1950, when my front doorbell rang and a Western Union messenger handed me a telegram containing the following terse order:

"LTJG S.MELVIN RINES X YOU ARE RECALLED TO ACTIVE DUTY X REPORT TO NAS GLENVIEW ILLINOIS AT 0800 ON 21 JULY 1950 X COMMANDING OFFICER."

I was already three days late. It was a total surprise. I had received no telephone call, no warning, and had seen nothing in the press about a call-up of reserves. I wired back:

"COMMANDING OFFICER NAS GLENVIEW X RECEIVED ORDERS TO ACTIVE DUTY THIS DATE X REQUEST FOUR DAYS TO WIND UP PERSONAL AFFAIRS X LTJG S MELVIN RINES"

Within hours, I received the following response:

"LTJG S. MELVIN RINES X REQUEST DENIED X REPORT NAS GLENVIEW ILLINOIS 0800 25 JULY 1950 X COMMANDING OFFICER"

I wired back that it was impossible to reach Glenview from northern New Hampshire by 0800 the next morning, and still in a negotiating mode, requested two days to wind up personal affairs. That evening, I received a telephone call from one of my squadron mates, saying, "Mel, where the hell are you? VF-721 has been recalled to active duty. You're listed as AWOL." He went on to say that the entire squadron was being airlifted to San Diego in two days and added, not entirely gratuitously, "You had better get your ass out here before we leave." "Tell them I'm on my way," I said and started packing.

The next morning, I was driven to North Conway (about thirty miles south of Berlin) to board an early train to Boston. From there I caught a plane to Chicago's Midway Airport on the south side and took a long and expensive taxi ride to Glenview in time to check into bachelors officers' quarters late that night. At 0800 the next morning, I officially reported in and was whisked down to the flight line, luggage in hand, where the entire squadron, officers and enlisted men, were gathered on the tarmac, waiting to load their gear aboard four navy R4D transport planes parked nearby.

I received a friendly but subdued welcome from my squadron mates, who were standing in small groups, talking quietly. They seemed almost stunned, still reeling from hasty good-byes to families, lovers, and friends. Many of them had left young or soon-to-be-born children, homes half-built, and promising careers just getting underway. By comparison, my situation was considerably less traumatic, although the abruptness and speed of the call-up was unsettling.

Everyone had a story to tell. Harry Peck, executive officer of the squadron, was the first to be called at his office in downtown Chicago and brusquely informed that VF-721 had been activated; and he was ordered to report for duty in one hour. When he arrived, he was charged with notifying the rest of the squadron to report immediately by any means possible. He set up a small group of people to telephone, wire telegrams, and when necessary, engage state and local police to find those not otherwise reachable. The navy was determined to prove that the ready reserve was, in fact, ready.

Most of us were reached by telephone or telegram. But one squadron member recounted, "I was fishing in the middle of a lake in northern Wisconsin on the first day of my vacation. It was early morning and very quiet when suddenly I heard an outboard motor start up in the distance. Mildly disturbed, I saw a small motorboat come into view and thought it was just another fisherman. As he got closer, I noticed he was in uniform and was bearing down on me; and I decided he must be a game warden. Instead, he turned out to be a forest ranger with the navy's order for me to report to NAS Glenview immediately." Another one told me, "I was driving along a highway, a little over the speed limit, when I saw the flashing lights of a state trooper behind me. I was initially relieved when, instead of a ticket he handed me a navy envelope from Glenview—until I opened it and the gravity of the message sunk in." Others were farther away on vacation or business trips and had to be tracked down through friends and relatives. None were missed. Thus began the saga of the first Naval Reserve Fighter Squadron in the country to be called up for active duty in the Korean War.

We started boarding the aircraft about forty-five minutes later, quietly filing up the steps, gear in hand. There was little of the boisterous camaraderie usually present when we were together. Not long after takeoff, however, our sober, individual reflections on leave-taking gradually shifted to thoughts of the future; and a group sense of excitement and adventure began to seep in. I was particularly pleased to be reunited with old friends, and of course, thrilled at the prospect of getting back in the air.

We landed at North Island Naval Air Station outside of San Diego after a back-breaking ten-hour flight in the transport's bucket seats. Those "seats" were little more than a line of shallow twenty-inch-wide indentations in aluminum benches lining each side of the plane. With no cushions and no backs and piles of baggage and other gear stacked in the middle, they made "economy class" luxurious in comparison.

As the plane taxied into our newly assigned operational area, we saw the finality of our recall playfully confirmed by a large banner draped over the hangar doors. It read WELCOME, WEEKEND WARRIORS with a large X painted across the WEEKEND. Less than five years had passed since I'd left this same base, expecting a future without war and quietly lamenting I would never fly a jet like the Ryan Fireball.

We settled in that night and jumpstarted operations in a blur of activity and confusion early the next morning. There were offices to move into, maintenance areas to be found, and equipment to be sorted and stowed. We made contact with other squadrons called up with us, a new air group command was established, and communication systems were installed, and so on. Amazingly, by the end of the day, the haze of confusion began to lift; and somehow the squadron began to function.

A "Ready Reserve Squadron" was, by definition, expected to be organized and trained to go into action at a moment's notice, the pilots combat ready, and the supporting specialists equipped to operate as soon as deployed. The transformation of this group of civilians, so recently engaged in diverse peacetime occupations, into an operational fighter squadron largely met those expectations—except that my squadron had no planes to fly.

Our F8Fs were left in Glenview because we had been told we would receive F4U Corsairs, the famed World War II fighter now demoted to air-to-ground combat, in San Diego. While we waited for them, word filtered down that we might be assigned the new jet-powered F9F-2 Panther still in production at Grumman Aircraft. It seemed almost too good to be true, but soon it was official: we would join that small band of elite carrier-based fighter pilots flying jets. In the meantime, we would train in Corsairs along with two other squadrons in the air group—the third having been assigned Skyraiders, a new single-engine bomber built by Douglas Aircraft.

The excitement generated by the introduction of jet-powered aircraft in the late 1940s and early '50s is difficult to recapture. These strange planes without propellers were just arriving at military bases and were years away from flying commercially, so few people had actually seen or heard one. Those who did were awed by their speed and deafened by the thunderous sound of their engines. The first operational fighter produced was the Air Force F-80, aptly named Thunder Jet; and it sounded very much like a thunder clap as it flashed by, leaving prolonged reverberations in the sky.

Propeller-driven airliners, on the other hand, were still flying at their customary low altitudes and slow speeds, making cross-country flights a grueling experience of refueling stops, flying through rather than over turbulent weather, and endless delays circling over congested airports, waiting to land. Still well in the future were the huge commercial jet planes that would climb high in the sky, quietly transporting hundreds of passengers to distant cities in less time than it took them to drive to their airport.

For a precious few military pilots, however, the future was now. Wearing Buck Rogers-style crash helmets and antigravity flight suits, jet pilots were streaking through the sky at what were then unimaginable speeds and altitudes. Their exploits were glamorized in movies and magazines and generated a level of public interest comparable to the first astronauts of a later day. And, of course, we couldn't wait to become one of them. But wait we did, for several months, causing the entire air group to miss an earlier departure date to Korea while we went through the motions of combat training in Corsairs.

When the first F9Fs arrived, my squadron mates and I gathered around in awe to touch (caress?) them, clamber into their cockpits, and over the following weeks, methodically study their operating and weapons systems. We had to learn totally new techniques to deal with high speeds, maximum Gs and possible engine flameouts, and how and when to eject when in trouble. In the latter case, a mock ejection seat was created and attached to two steel rails pointing straight up and armed with an explosive charge beneath it.

After being told what to expect, I strapped in, braced myself, and pulled a canvas windshield down over my face that, in turn, fired the charge. Almost instantly I found myself at the top of those rails, staring down some twenty-five or thirty feet. An actual ejection would be preceded by jettisoning the canopy, and when in the air, unbuckling the seat and pulling the ripcord to open the parachute—a time-consuming procedure requiring hundreds of feet in altitude to accomplish. Today, everything is automatic and almost instantaneous, and the seats are rocket propelled, making it possible to eject safely with zero altitude and/or zero airspeed. No matter, this system was far superior to the old method of scrambling out of a cockpit, in hurricane winds, hoping to clear the tail section before pulling the ripcord.

Most of the training for high-altitude flight conditions was conducted on the ground in a pressure chamber. A group of us, equipped with oxygen masks, were seated in the chamber, and among other things were told of the perils of anoxia (too little oxygen). The instructor asked for a volunteer to take off his mask at the equivalent of twenty thousand feet and do a few simple tasks. I raised my hand and was seated at a table with a cardboard box with a slot in the top, and a pack of cards. The airtight door was slammed shut, and the pressure started to drop.

When the pressure-measuring altimeter read twenty thousand feet, I was instructed to remove my mask and put one card at a time through the slot. No problem, I thought. In fact, I not only did it easily; I seemed to get better at it as I went along. I was so pleased with myself that I even began imagining their amazement at my ability to perform without oxygen and the praise about to be heaped on me—when I regained consciousness. Once the instructor replaced my mask and I had taken a few breaths, I saw the table strewn with cards, many that had landed on the floor. I couldn't believe it; I was sure they were all going neatly into the box! I had experienced the classic diabolical symptoms of anoxia: burgeoning confidence, a progressive feeling of well-being, just as my judgment was rapidly declining. The lesson was clear and long lasting.

Beyond these training sessions and the usual ground-school studies on operating systems and procedures, everything else had to be learned in the air— alone, for the navy still had no two-seater fighters or jet trainers. I had grown used to this while checking out in other fighters, and generally didn't sweat it; but this would be different, I would be flying a plane vastly different from anything I had flown before, at speeds and altitudes never experienced.

Reality seldom matches the anticipation of major events, but this time it did. Just getting strapped and plugged in, taxiing to the duty runway, firmly applying brakes, and tentatively pushing the throttle forward to 100 percent power was a rush. The first surprise was the eerie quiet in the cockpit even though the rising roar of the engine was deafening to the surrounding countryside. The second surprise was when I released my brakes and nothing much happened, in sharp contrast to the surge and rapid acceleration produced by a propeller-driven fighter.

The Panther just started rolling slowly, gradually accelerating as the runway ahead got shorter and shorter. As my speed rose, more and more air was being rammed into the engine, producing ever more power, further increasing the rate of acceleration, devouring the remaining runway faster and faster. Long past the point where a propeller plane would be airborne, and with little left of the six-thousand-foot runway, I finally reached flying speed and gently lifted off. For the next few minutes, I gingerly manipulated the stick and rudders, learning to coordinate the highly sensitive, hydraulically boosted control surfaces (another first) as I zoomed to twenty thousand feet.

The sensations of speed and free flight were exhilarating, to say the least, especially when sitting in the nose of an aircraft, under a bubble canopy, with the engine and wings aft and out of sight. Everything happened quicker, quieter, and smoother than anything I'd experienced before. I felt more like a passenger than the pilot in control as the Panther flew at speeds and altitudes seldom reached in conventional aircraft. I started out with shallow turns, mild dives, and climbs, and experimented with various power and trim settings. I slowed down and lowered wheels and flaps and noted sink rates when raised. Eventually, I just relaxed and watched the landscape sweep by below. By the end of the hour, the initial strangeness had slipped gradually into a mildly comfortable feeling of familiarity and confidence—even dominance.

Landing a jet, although certainly different, was in some ways easier than landing a prop. To be sure, it required a flatter approach, a wider turn, and higher speeds, but that was balanced by better visibility and a tricycle landing gear obviating the exquisitely timed three-point landing required for conventional fighters. My approach and landing were just OK, but taxiing back was far less tentative than going out; along with increased confidence, I could hardly wait to get back to the flight line where a minireception was sure to be waiting. I jumped down from the cockpit to greet well-wishing squadron mates, and in my excitement, hugged our grizzled chief boson's mate, the top noncommissioned officer in our squadron (and stickler for military protocol)—to his embarrassment and mine.

As soon as we got checked out in the new planes, training went into high gear. Although the rudiments of formation flying, dive bombing, strafing, and dogfighting remained the same, everything had to be relearned in a jet. Speeds, of course, were greater; but the radius of turns and the airspace required for maneuvers such as loops, split Ss, and bombing runs were vastly increased. We were startled to find, for example, that two of us could circle over an agreed rendezvous point and still not see each other—until we figured out how to deal with the plane's huge turning radius.

When dogfighting, the high altitudes, closing speeds of over a thousand knots, and more punishing G-forces made wholly new demands on our bodies. A typical fight would begin at twenty thousand feet with two jets flying directly at each other while maintaining one thousand feet in altitude separation. The fight was on as soon as the planes crossed, giving the pilot at the higher altitude the tactical advantage. He typically would turn sharply in an attempt to get behind the adversary flashing by beneath him. The disadvantaged pilot, in defense, had to turn immediately in the opposite direction or become a dead duck almost before the fight began. Thereafter, each would try to turn inside the other by making turns tighter and faster and by pulling higher and higher Gs without blacking out, in order to bring his guns to bear on the other's tail. Victory ultimately belonged to the pilot who had the skill and courage to cross in front of the other in the ever-tightening scissors and endure the most G-forces.

Dogfighting was, of course, the sine qua non of a fighter pilot, demanding skills and courage separating him from all other flyers. I worked hard at it, eventually mastered it, and forever reveled in it. The aerial scenes in the movie *Top Gun* captured much of the high-speed drama as Tom Cruise et al. tried to outmaneuver adversaries in simulated combat. However, artistic license added sound effects in cockpits where none were heard, depicted tactics that would be fatal if flown, and showed pilots in violent maneuvers looking remarkably fresh and unburdened by the grueling forces of gravity.

In real life, we wore skintight G-suits that prolonged consciousness by inflating bladders strategically placed throughout the body, especially in the gut, slowing the flow of blood from the brain. The suit was attached to a compressed air system that instantly increased and released pressure in the bladders as Gs varied. In a dogfight, with its rapid and abrupt changes in G forces, the constant pummeling from pressure changes, and constant effort just to hold one's head up and back straight, took its toll. After an hour or so of simulated combat, the smiling and relaxed Tom Cruise and friends would, in fact, have been "wrung out" and exhausted by the unremitting tension.

A young jet fighter pilot, especially one headed for combat, almost by definition lived fast and dangerously each day (and well into the night) with little thought of the future. I doubt any of us really thought we would die—I know I certainly didn't—but all of us were aware of the heightened possibility, and that was sufficient reason (or perhaps excuse) to "eat, drink, and be merry" whenever we could. We had our favorite bars in Coronado and San Diego where aviators hung out and single women congregated. And of course, favorite restaurants, such as the Mexican Village just outside the main gate where the food was good, the beer cold, and aviators abounded. But for squadron bachelors, Mecca on weekends was Palm Springs, a three-hour drive over the mountains into the desert.

In 1950, Palm Springs was a small town with upscale stores and a few restaurants lining a main street running through its center. Off that street were roads leading into areas of lush homes, a few small inns, a golf course, and a couple of tennis clubs. Only ninety minutes from Los Angeles, it had become the playground of Hollywood stars. I was a charter member of the squadron bachelors who regularly drove over the mountains whenever we had the chance. Other regulars were Charlie Leary, Whitey Lichtfuss, Jocko Schlosser, and Pogo McGraw, plus an occasional stray lured by our lurid stories. We customarily rented a unit at the Villa Hermosa, a small complex of villas surrounding a large swimming pool. The cost, when divided by our number, was quite reasonable; and it immediately became our weekend headquarters for almost nonstop partying.

The glamour imparted by our uniforms apparently offset any complaints about boisterous behavior, for the proprietor always seemed happy to see us. We soon learned that *the* place to go on Saturday nights was the ultraexclusive Racquet Club, owned by Charles Farrell, a famous retired silent-film actor and present mayor of Palm Springs. It was truly the hangout of the stars, but how to get in? The policy was strictly Members Only, which of course we were not, and we didn't know anyone who was.

I happened to see a local newspaper account of a celebrity party at the club hosted by a Mrs. Grace Pope ("doyen of hostesses" it called her), and I noted her name. Saturday night, resplendent in our blue uniforms, gold braid, and wings, four of us drove up to the secluded entrance to the club; and I strolled over to the doorman. I introduced myself and informed him that we were guests of Mrs. Pope and wondered if she had arrived. Serendipity reigned for she had actually made reservations for that night and hadn't yet arrived. But (surprise, surprise) "she didn't mention any guests." My good-natured understanding of the oversight was soon laced with thinly veiled irritation as the doorman tried to figure out what to do with us.

He quickly suggested we wait for her at the bar just inside the entrance. From there we soon melted in with the large Saturday-night crowd of members and guests, many of whom, as billed, were well-known movie stars. Because it was an exclusive enclave, their conduct tended to be more relaxed, so it was interesting to see them at play and often difficult to reconcile their actions with their screen personas. The sophisticated and mature Academy Award-winning star of *Mrs. Minniver*, for example, could be seen dancing a wild Charleston as the real life Greer Garson. Richard Widmark, a gangster fresh from pushing an old woman in a wheelchair down a flight of stairs, had turned into a friendly but shy ex-school teacher. And the irrepressible Groucho Marx couldn't resist asking how everything was going in the *army* as we stood at adjoining urinals in the men's room—and greeted my exaggerated outrage with his trademark dancing eyebrows.

We were having a marvelous time and feeling very relaxed when an attractive, rather mature woman approached me and asked my name. "Lieutenant Mel

Rines," I responded. "Oh, how nice to meet you, Lieutenant," she said with a twinkle in her eye. "I am Grace Pope. I am so pleased you and your friends could join me as my guests this evening." It was the beginning of a wonderful friendship for she loved our boldness and seemed to enjoy the novelty and glamour of high-flying jet-fighter pilots around her. She invited us to parties at her lovely home and for other evenings at the Racquet Club where greetings from the doorman had miraculously become effusive.

On one such visit, I met William Holden and his dazzling wife, Brenda Marshall, and we wound up having dinner and spending most of the evening together. Ms. Marshall, also in the movies, was a breathtaking classic beauty with jet-black hair and pale white skin; but on that evening at least, she seemed cold and remote. Holden paid scant attention to her as he and I talked—and drank—long into the night. His easygoing personality and understated charm were much the same off screen as on and our conversation ranged widely, but a lot of it had to do with flying jets in the navy. I sensed he was a frustrated would-be fighter pilot, not entirely content to play roles in movies instead of real life. Years later, in the film *The Bridges at Toko-Ri,* he also was a naval reservist recalled to fly Panthers off a carrier in Korea; and I had to wonder if our conversation had anything to do with it.

Another evening, I met a sparkling blonde starlet named Mona Freeman who often played what she was in real life: an early-twenties ingénue around whom handsome young men flocked. We enjoyed each other's company, dancing and kidding around; and she asked me to be her tennis partner the next afternoon against William Powell and his wife. I had to decline because I was flying a twin-engine Beechcraft with limited ceiling and preferred flying through mountain passes in daylight rather than over them at night. However, she invited me to meet her on the set of *Dear Brat,* a movie she had just started, in Hollywood. As it happened, Joe Quirk, the squadron armaments officer and former pilot, and I had already arranged a trip to Hollywood to ask the Disney Studios to design a logo for our squadron. I made a date to visit her after that meeting.

Disney agreed to help and designed a knight in armor on horseback, fiercely charging forward to pierce a red star with his lance—and our squadron name became "Starbusters." This they did gratis, with no credit or publicity of any kind. We joined Mona the next day and watched her do an interminable number of "takes" for a scene with Edward Arnold playing her father. In it, she was supposed to have misbehaved and her "father" chased, caught, scolded, and shook her. She responded by kicking him in the shins and running away. "Cut," the director shouted, "let's do it again." They kept repeating the scene, a thirty-second sequence at most, to correct something or another, and she kept kicking him. During a break, I asked Arnold how his leg was holding up. "Okay," he grinned and pulled up the pant leg to reveal a baseball catcher's shin guard. Other scenes, equally short and painfully repeated, suggested glamour in movie making was more imaginary than real. But Mona was relaxed, gracious, and posed for pictures with us during breaks then miraculously reverted to a young brat and went back to work.

Late that afternoon, with time on our hands, we drove to the Beverly Hills Hotel for a beer at the bar. While sitting there, I noted a great amount of activity swirling around the hotel apparently in preparation for a big event and asked the bartender what was going on. "It's the biggest night of the year, the Press Photographers' Ball," he said, "all the big stars are coming." "Is there anyway we can get in?" I asked. "Not a chance. You'd need a written invitation, and there'll be security guards all over the place to stop crashers," he snapped back. It sounded like a challenge to me—and I accepted.

After finishing our beers and freshening up, we walked outside to watch the early arrivals and case the situation. Like most well-publicized Hollywood events, there was a long line of black limousines slowly approaching the heavily guarded entrance bathed in floodlights. When reached, attendants leapt forward to open doors, celebrities stepped out on a red carpet and walked between velvet ropes into the hotel, as cameras flashed and crowds strained to catch a glimpse of them. It was all very interesting—and daunting. Suddenly, I thought, "Black!" Quirk's car is black. To be sure, it was only a Chevrolet sedan, but it would have to do. We got into his car and entered the line of block-long limousines as they inched toward the entrance, not sure how we would be received. Upon arrival, the attendants flung open the doors; and we strolled regally between the hallowed ropes, nodding graciously to the crowd, and with flashbulbs popping, entered the hotel.

So far so good, we were inside the hotel, but not in the ballroom where invitations were being scrupulously checked at the door. I spotted Hoagy Carmichael standing near the entrance, with two luscious young blondes in tow. Remembering he also was a member of Kappa Sigma fraternity, I walked over, introduced myself, and told him we still sang "My Kappa Sigma Sweetheart" (which he wrote) to our dates at all fraternity parties. He was mildly pleased. Then I went on to explain our situation, our grand entrance, and that we were trying to figure out how to get into the party without an invitation. He loved the story and quickly offered a plan: "I'll lead the way, and you each take one of my friends and follow me." We barely acknowledged the guards' presence as we talked animatedly with our ladies on the way by.

After thanking Hoagy and exchanging an exaggerated secret fraternity handshake, we parted and looked around for a table to join. Stars were everywhere—dressed, coifed, and made up to look their best for the photographers. Harriet and Ozzie Nelson invited us to share their table with Janet Leigh and her new husband, Tony Curtis. After an intense picture-taking session, the photographers were ushered out; and the party began in earnest. There was dancing, more than a little drinking, and nonstop table-hopping, as headline entertainers performed, many with improvised routines not seen before or probably since. They ran the gamut of Hollywood's top talent, but Danny Kaye was easily the most engaging, with his incredible range of material and irrepressible joy in performing.

As navy officers, we enjoyed sufficient status to mingle easily with the guests, and took advantage of it. Our table mate, Tony Curtis, dashing and preening with his well-oiled hair and deep tan, revealed the insecurity of a new actor dazzled by growing celebrity, and overwhelmed by the training and promotion required by his studio. Janet Leigh, more experienced, joined in to explain details of the star system and some of its less-glamorous aspects. Ozzie and Harriet played Ozzie and Harriet, the down-to earth neighbors-next-door types enjoying real conversations.

Glancing around the room, I saw an uncharacteristically plump Sonja Heine pouring a drink from a flask in her purse, and watched Nicky Hilton, with too much to drink, wandering around the dance floor, ignoring his new bride, Elizabeth Taylor. I chatted briefly with Gene Tierney, easily the most beautiful woman in the room, and joined in the dancing—some spirited, but most relatively restrained. One of my partners was Elizabeth Taylor, beautiful and disarming in her late teen years, wholly engaged in her career. She frequently greeted other guests around us with, "Are you working?" as though they might otherwise be on welfare. The question suggested a constant worry about new roles as soon as the last one was finished, even among the brightest stars.

Between sets, while waiting for the music to begin again, Taylor engaged another starlet in a mildly risqué conversation, possibly for my benefit, on the virtues of East-West bras vs. whatever kind produced the cleavage she was so famous for. I strained mightily to avoid looking directly at the examples before me, and deemed it politic to refrain from stating a preference. And so it went all evening: interesting and dazzling women everywhere. I hardly remember any men.

Back at the base, training accelerated, highlighted by a temporary move of the entire squadron to NAS El Centro, located in the heart of the California desert. This phase, lasting about a month, consisted of virtually around-the-clock flying. It was an earlier version of the navy's Top Gun School, designed to polish fighter tactics, gunnery, and rocket-firing techniques, and raise our proficiency in instrument and night flying. There were dummy tanks and vehicles to bomb and strafe, towed target sleeves to make gunnery runs on, and constant dog-fighting that grew in intensity and risk.

By this time, I had become one with the Panther; its engine was my heartbeat, its nose, wings, and tail, my being. I maneuvered without thinking, and was relaxed and comfortable climbing, diving, or inverted—alone or in formation. I felt confident to the point of being fearless, ready to take on any contingency—a supremely wonderful state of being.

I remember one night in particular, climbing well above thirty thousand feet to bask in the darkness and exult in the solitude of a star-studded universe, disturbed only by the faint glow of my instruments. I trimmed the plane so finely that merely shifting my weight caused a wing dip, and let my mind drift back to those youthful dreams of a wannabe fighter pilot—the play-acting, the passion. Yet, I had never imagined the ecstasy of this moment, silently slipping through space, in total control—and alone. Reality had dwarfed the dream.

We carried three rockets on each wing and four twenty-millimeter cannons in the nose—greater firepower on a more stable platform than any propeller-driven fighter. And we were constantly striving to improve accuracy. This was not easy because our gun sights still relied on our judgment of rapidly changing distances, speeds, and angles of attack, and our accuracy was totally dependent on the stability of the platform at the time of firing. Heat-seeking rockets, guided missiles, and smart bombs steered after firing were still far in the future. Gradually, with practice (and some amazement) I developed a high degree of accuracy, hitting those tanks and peppering those sleeves while maneuvering in every configuration. Another stage of readiness and confidence was reached.

The squadron's basic unit was the four-plane division, made up of two-plane sections. Positions within the division were largely determined by seniority, the date of commissioning. My division was led by Jim Dodge, solid, steady, and accomplished; and his wingman, Whitey Lichtfuss, outspoken, a quick study, and the squadron jokester. Charlie Leary was my section leader, a happy, story-telling Irishman with a keen lawyer's mind, and I, junior but unbowed, his wingman. We developed a bond unmatched by any other social experience, enduring more than a half century despite long separations.

We always flew together, constantly trying to improve our performance to confirm what we already knew: WE WERE THE BEST OF THE BEST. But then, so were the other divisions, they thought. The competition devolved down to the little things: the tightest formation, most spectacular breakup to landing, most daring tail-chase. It even extended to the radio checks immediately after takeoff. It was "Jimbo over to Whitey," "Over to Charlie," "Back to Jimbo," rapid fire, in a fraction of a second. No pauses permitted.

The time finally arrived when we had only to become carrier qualified in jets to be declared combat ready—but there were no carriers available for such training on the West Coast. I almost welcomed the news for it was now late December, with the holidays approaching, and I could use a break. But it was not to be. We were loaded aboard the *Constitution*, a huge propeller-driven navy transport, briefly noted for being the world's largest passenger plane, with more than two hundred seats on two complete levels. We were flown nonstop to Jacksonville, arriving in terrible weather, and had to sweat out three aborted landing attempts before finally setting down.

The next day, New Year's Eve, we were bused to the port, embarked in a large landing craft, and pushed off to rendezvous with the USS *Oriskany*, one of the largest carriers in the fleet at the time. It was cold even in Florida, the seas were rough, and the rendezvous was delayed for hours while we circled in the assigned area, waiting for the ship to appear. Standing in this pitching and rolling bargelike boat, in full uniform and overcoat, and being drenched periodically by sea spray did little for my disposition.

When the huge carrier finally loomed into view, the sea was too rough to board via its platform, so the ship's crew lowered steel nets over the side for us to climb. It was a long, cold, cumbersome, dark, and dangerous fifty-foot climb up to the pitching deck, all the while being egged on by playful shouts of "Happy New Year" by the ship's crew above. It didn't help at all when we learned the planes we were using belonged to a regular (career) navy squadron whose pilots had gone home for the holidays!

Flying jets off a carrier was considerably different from flying conventional aircraft. The jet's higher landing speed, increased turning radius, lagged response to power changes, and increased fuel consumption required major adjustments. And, of course, they had to be catapulted rather than flown off the deck to get airborne. The pilot's improved visibility, especially when landing and taxiing, was a small compensating factor. Again, with a single-seat fighter, there was no way to experience the blinding acceleration of a catapult takeoff, or the instant deceleration of an arrested landing except by doing it—alone—and it had to be right the first time for there were no second chances. Catapult takeoffs were especially daunting. I had never made one, and it's impossible to imagine what it's like from someone else's description.

After strapping in and making a long list of control and engine checks, I taxied into position near the forward part of the flight deck. There, a steel cable ("bridle") was attached to my underbelly and the other end fastened to a metal hook protruding from a recessed track running to the end of the flight deck. The hook was attached to a huge hydraulically powered shaft encased in a cylinder running just below the flight deck. With hookup complete and checked, a heat shield rose slowly behind my plane to deflect the coming holocaust of exhaust from my tailpipe.

The catapult officer took over, and holding up one finger, twirled his arm faster and faster above his head, signaling a run-up to full power for a final high-pressure pump test. With the engine roaring, I snapped the throttle back to half power, causing the primary pump to shut down and a red light to go on. If the light goes out within two seconds it means the backup pump has taken over and I will be cleared to go; longer, and I must abort the take off. When I signaled the pumps were working, the cat officer showed two fingers, and started twirling his outstretched arm faster and faster until the engine was back at full power.

Bracing for the shot, I took one last glance at my instruments, and gave him a pronounced salute. With the jet screaming and straining against its bridle, the cat officer went into a crouch, dramatically pointing his outstretched arm forward, signaling LAUNCH. But nothing happened. The engine was roaring at full blast, my head was back against the headrest, left hand encircled a post at full-throttle position, right hand on stick with elbow planted in my gut for support, and feet pressed against the rudder pedals—and I wait.

But there's no turning back: at the cat officer's signal, a seaman at the edge of the deck pressed a button, switching on a red light below that signaled another seaman to throw a lever, unleashing the hydraulic shaft. Suddenly, with a startling whoosh, the plane lept forward, streaked down the track, accelerating to over 110 knots (126 miles per hour) in eighty feet, and I shot off the deck. As my mind cleared, the feel of the controls and a glance at my instruments confirmed that I was safely airborne.

We practiced landings and catapulted takeoffs for the rest of the week without incident, and were officially designated carrier qualified in jets. The *Oriskany* returned to port, we disembarked, and finally, were given a short post-New Year's leave. We were told we would ship out to Korea upon our return.

CHAPTER 8

"THE GREATEST SHOW
ON EARTH"

Of course, all ships appear larger when docked than at sea, but I was stunned to see the gargantuan aircraft carrier placidly sitting there, with its huge flight deck and massive superstructure towering over the landscape. Gazing upward, I felt diminished by its sheer bulk and stolid bearing, and found it difficult to believe it was actually floating. But floating it was, and it had just become my new home—the USS *Boxer*, CV-21. Weighing more than thirty-five thousand tons, with a thirty-foot draft, and a flight deck more than three football fields long, it slept, fed, and cared for thirty-five hundred souls. Along with the basics for life at sea, there were barbershops, laundries, a medical clinic, and space for an occasional movie or basketball game. It carried more than one hundred warplanes onboard, with all the equipment necessary to service, fuel, arm, and maintain them in all-weather conditions, while plowing through the world's oceans at speeds in excess of thirty knots.

When I arrived, the *Boxer* was monumentally engaged in the organized chaos of going to sea. An endless stream of vehicles wound its way to the dock, bringing supplies of every description to be loaded on conveyer belts and deposited throughout the ship. Overhead, huge towering cranes hoisted planes, helicopters, and other heavy equipment onto the flight deck. The area was swarming with seamen and their officious supervisors, armed with clipboards, busily checking off everything in sight. The wonder was that anyone could plan, much less stow, all the equipment, ammunition, food, water, and personal items required for so many people and aircraft on an extended cruise at sea.

Our personal preparations, on the other hand, were minimal. Uniforms and flight gear were, of course, prescribed for us, and there was little space to stow much else. I was still a junior officer, and the quarters assigned me matched my rank: "Boys' Town," where rows of bunks stacked three high were interspersed with individual all-purpose cabinets incorporating a desk, storage shelves, and drawers. Mine was a top bunk where the air was a little clearer but space more limited—just six inches between my head and a large overhead asbestos-covered pipe. I was also directly below a catapult that frequently overwhelmed the hum of the ship with a whoosh and a roar without warning. I threw my bags on the bunk and went topside to watch the final loading, and growing number of people assembling on the dock to bid us farewell.

Inexorably, the time to ship out arrived; dock lines were released, and the waving began, first tentatively then more vigorously, between families and friends. There was a pervading undertone of sadness onboard even though far below flags were flying, a navy band was playing, and the crowd, mostly women and children, continued to wave enthusiastically. I watched quietly as the *Boxer* slid slowly from the dock, and the waving petered out, the band broke up, and the crowd began to drift off. Somber though it seemed, we were the lucky ones with adventures and new experiences awaiting us, while those waving below would wend their way back to homes now strangely empty, to wait and worry. Lost in thought, I went below to begin a new life at sea.

Some of my squadron mates had extended carrier duty in World War II, and loved to tell the neophytes among us what it was like and what to expect. Charlie Leary (whom I frequently referred to as my wingman, although I was actually his) took a special delight in explaining the social dynamics of life aboard ship. He told me in all seriousness, "Mel, beware of rumors, they'll be everywhere. I guarantee someone will tell you he just heard the cruise was being cut short and we're returning home. And he'll give you an unimpeachable source with all the reasons why."

Charlie was right, for about four days after getting underway he rushed up to me and said, "Mel, I just learned we're heading back to dry dock, one of the engines is malfunctioning." I remained unmoved, and replied, "It's probably just one of those rumors you warned me about." He said, "No, no, this one is true. I heard it from a chief petty officer who has a friend working in the engine room." Charlie's source notwithstanding, we kept going west and he never mentioned it again. "Irritations," he also said, "are bound to occur even between the nicest guys, and for the most insignificant reasons." I was reminded of his prophecy when about three months into the cruise, I was intensely bothered by an otherwise good friend who slathered TOO DAMN MUCH BUTTER on his toast every morning.

Paradoxically, none of the reminiscences of WWII involved heroics, planes shot down, or disasters averted. It would take half a century (our squadron's fiftieth reunion), before I learned that Bob Duncan, one of our division leaders, had shot down four Japanese planes in one swirling dogfight—and then only because he was asked to relate the story for a squadron video. And that Harry Peck, our executive officer, had been shot down in the South Pacific, spent hours in the water before rescue, and returned to his squadron to fight again. This only came out in an unrelated conversation.

But perhaps the most astonishing of all was the news clipping I recently received about a WWII ace named Joseph D. McGraw, who had five confirmed kills, three "probables," and three damaged, and had been awarded a Navy Cross, Distinguished Flying Cross, and eight Air Medals in WWII. Joe and I shared many bachelor soirees in Palm Springs and Japan, almost a year aboard ship, and countless hours traveling by car—and he never mentioned it.

Our immediate attention was focused on Hawaii where we were scheduled to engage in an intense operations readiness exercise in which the entire carrier air group and ship's company would work together for the first time. Our all-reserve air group, CAG 101, was composed of three squadrons of dive bombers (two flying Corsairs and one Skyraiders), along with my fighter squadron of Panthers, totaling approximately one hundred airplanes. There was also a photo reconnaissance group flying four unarmed, specially equipped Panthers, and a six-plane "night heckler" bombing unit in Corsairs. A helicopter for air-sea rescues rounded out the aircraft inventory.

Putting all the maintenance, armament, fueling, and ship-handling crews together and fitting them into complex systems of an aircraft carrier with its intricate deck and air operations was challenging, to say the least. But like preseason training for a sports team, initial confusion progressed through mild disorganization, to a system of "plays" to study and practice until perfected and ingrained. There was no other way.

We went through our repertory of bombing and strafing runs using a towed target sled, conducted air-to-air combat maneuvers, and of course, made multiple landings on the carrier. At the same time, the *Boxer's* crew was busy spotting, launching, and recovering aircraft, and firing its own antiaircraft guns at towed targets as it polished its navigational and defensive skills. Every operation was observed, timed, and graded by the fleet-appointed independent inspection team over a four-day examination period. The exercise was impressive, and proceeded almost without incident until one pilot, the air group executive officer, was unable to extend his tail hook, and waited too long before heading for an airfield at Pearl Harbor.

He almost made it. His engine flamed out just short of the runway and he crash-landed in a heavily wooded area. The plane was a total loss, but he miraculously survived almost unscathed. This accident, however, turned out only to be "strike one"—a harbinger of problems to come. "Strike two" occurred while operating off Korea. He got too slow in his approach to a landing on the carrier, stalled out, and plunged into the sea. Fortunately, the helicopter plucked him—again, shaken but uninjured—out of the plane just before it sank.

Ordinarily, this would have been cause for grounding, at least temporarily, but as executive officer of a combat air group, his career was on a fast track, and he was allowed to continue flying. "Strike three" was called over Korea when he fixated on target and flew through the tops of trees on his pullout. He barely made it back to the carrier. Later, as I listened to his story in the ready room, he was shaking so badly the coffee cup rattled in his hand, spilling coffee in the saucer. He was grounded for the cruise and likely for good, ending his hopes for a naval career. I doubt he argued otherwise.

We were declared "Operational Ready," and celebrated with a long night of partying at Waikiki Beach. The next day, 17 March 1951 (which, Charlie had to point out, "honored a venerable Irish Saint"), we headed for Korea, grateful for hangover-recovery time. The next ten days were primarily devoted to "business": poring over maps, checking gear, reviewing operational codes and procedures, and responding to calls to "General Quarters" at least once a day (or night). These calls, preceded by a deafening Klaxon, were broadcast throughout the ship, urgently repeated over and over again.

They demanded, and never failed to receive, maximum attention. Everybody aboard, more than three thousand men, dropped whatever they were doing and joined an intricate preplanned scramble to reach an individually assigned battle station. The need for speed was reinforced by the rapid, systematic slamming and locking of steel hatches by the last man through each passageway, making the ship's compartments water-tight, and trapping the tardy behind.

We plowed through a relatively calm Pacific Ocean, with few sightings of other ships or aircraft. The vastness of that great body of water and the insignificance of our presence upon it, even with the power and majesty of an aircraft carrier, was sobering. I wondered anew how sailors in the wooden vessels of old with no means of communication, no one to come to their rescue, imprecise navigation instruments, and afloat at the mercy of the weather, could challenge the power of that ocean for months on end. By contrast, our huge floating city was festooned with radio and radar gear, in constant communication with other ships and aircraft, that were minutely aware of our position at all times.

Meanwhile, with no flight operations, I spent a great deal of the time reading, playing cards, exploring the ship, and taking long walks on the flight deck for exercise. Ready One, our squadron ready room, was pilot headquarters and all-purpose lounging and relaxing area. The officers' wardroom was dining room, library, and game room all rolled into one. And our bunks and adjoining desks provided occasional refuge from the intense, almost continuous social interaction. The routine, initially so exciting, gradually slipped into mild boredom as the novelty of being at sea subsided. But as we got closer to Korea, a palpable quickening of pace and mounting tension appeared throughout the ship, as we prepared to join the Sixth Fleet and begin air operations.

On 27 March 1951, specks appeared on the horizon and slowly materialized into ships—lots of them. We gradually identified an aircraft carrier and a cruiser, surrounded by fourteen destroyers, and although unseen, several submerged submarines as a protective screen. This was Task Force 77, a formidable array of battle-ready warships manned by some ten thousand men, imbuing immense confidence merely by being part of it.

The carrier we relieved had already departed, so we moved directly into position in the middle of the destroyer screen. Although adverse weather precluded immediate air operations, flight preparations got underway. The flight deck was "spotted" (planes arranged on deck in the number and order of takeoff), and all pilots reported to their ready rooms to check for scheduled missions, time of launch, and targets. Assignments were by four-plane divisions, and the personnel and positions in ours remained the same. We had trained together for months, knew each other's capabilities, and were good friends in the air and on the ground. Shared combat would now create bonds beyond those in any other life experience.

We were scheduled for an "armed reconnaissance" the next day along a well-defined, code-named route, and were thoroughly briefed on what to attack (anything that moved), what to expect (antiaircraft fire ranging from small arms to five-inch cannons), and what codes and communication protocols would be used that day. Other divisions would fan out over North Korea with the same overall purpose: to interdict enemy supplies to troops on the front lines. We were ready to go, but the weather stayed bad, and we waited. We rechecked the forecasts, went topside to look at the sky, and waited some more. And so it continued for the rest of that day and the next. But then the weather showed signs of improving; the forecast turned favorable.

We were scheduled for launch the next morning, 30 March, at the relatively civilized time of 8:00 a.m. (0800 in navy time). The curtain was about rise on what has been described as "the greatest show on earth," staged on a pitching, rolling deck, often in gale-force winds, always plunging through the world's oceans. As men and planes move into position, danger is everywhere: from whirling propellers and flaming exhausts, to loading and unloading bombs and rockets—all under the intense pressure of limited time and space. Men in colored T-shirts scurry in and around taxiing planes as they inch toward catapults, or come screaming over the ramp, slam down, catch a wire, and stop cold.

The underlying din is loud and constant, surpassed only by high-pitched shrieks of jets straining on a catapult, or full-throated roars from throttling up after landing. The unquestioned maestro directing this performance is Primary Fly (a.k.a. "Fly One" or "Air Boss") perched high above the flight deck on the carrier's bridge, issuing orders and giving directions by signal, radio, or bullhorn.

An air group launch is not unlike a giant chess game where disparate pieces (jets and prop planes) are carefully arranged (spotted) and moved in accordance with their configuration and power (fighters, dive bombers). The launching order is predetermined by type of mission assigned, amount of fuel required, and method of takeoff. It is played out on a moving deck, with little separation between jets and props as they taxi into position for launch. The air boss, using a public address system powerful enough to be heard above all else, directs every move. Time pressures are intense, no piece in this chess game is expendable, and no interruption or delay is allowed.

I reported to the already bustling ready room at 0600 the next morning, having slept well. After donning layers of flight gear, studying charts, reviewing frequencies and codes, and listening to a last-minute intelligence briefing, the room quieted down, and I sat in one of the leather "barbershop" chairs and waited. It was a time to contemplate, to be alone with one's thoughts, and deal with unresolved concerns. My mind was filled with healthy anticipation and a modicum of apprehension, but no fear. The big game, the one I had spent years training for, was about to start, and I felt confident and ready. Suddenly, all ruminating ceased, shattered by a loud speaker blaring: "Pilots, man your planes," and the room erupted. The time to think had passed. I rushed through the hatch, worked my way through a narrow passageway, and clambered up on deck.

There, I became an integral player in an elaborate and thunderous choreography of planes and men, culminating in being shot from a flight deck fifty-feet above a roiling sea. The deck was already pulsating with swarms of men clad in brightly colored T-shirts, going about their assigned tasks. Those in yellow shirts directed the movement of aircraft, purple shirts fueled them, red shirts armed and rushed to them if they crashed, and brown shirts, the plane captains, waited by their assigned planes to report its condition, and assist the pilot upon arrival.

I emerged heavily laden with helmet, oxygen mask, "Mae West," chart board, a notepad to clamp on my thigh, and a thirty-eight revolver on my hip. I strode briskly to my plane, listened to the plane captain's condition report, and walked around it, inspecting control surfaces and checking wing tanks, rocket attachments, and landing gear. Then, much as a squire prepared the knights of old for battle, the plane captain helped me climb up on the wing, settle into the cockpit, and get strapped, plugged and connected to various hoses and cords. When complete, he dismounted, and stood by my left wing until the order to start engines was received, and I turned my attention to a "yellow shirt" for directions.

The yellow shirt hand-signaled to release brakes, and guided me within inches of other planes as I slowly wove my way toward the catapult. It was quintessential stop-and-go traffic as I was passed along from yellow shirt to yellow shirt before finally breaking free and being positioned on the catapult. The crew quickly snapped the steel bridle to the plane's underbelly as the exhaust shield rose behind me. Then I turned my attention to the catapult officer. He held up one finger and twirled his arm faster and faster for the high-pressure fuel-pump check. At full power, I snapped the throttle back, and my panel light went on and off within the required two seconds. I was ready to go.

The cat officer showed two fingers, and twirled his arm rapidly as I went back to full power. Left hand around the throttle post, a last glance at my instruments, a pronounced hand salute, then he dropped to a crouch pointing his right arm forward, and the unstoppable launch sequence began. An interminable few seconds passed, and suddenly, I was slammed back in my seat, my vision blurred, and I was shot off the bow of the carrier. As my vision cleared, I glanced at my airspeed (110 knots), pulled the stick back into a climbing turn, and slid on to Charlie's wing.

Our mission: Destroy all traffic on a well-traveled supply route some fifty miles north of the front lines. Joined in tight formation, we headed for the "beach," with charts in place, and guns and rockets switched into firing position. It seemed almost surreal. Here I was, on a sunny Sunday morning, a time when I might otherwise be in church, and I was in a gleaming jet, armed to the teeth, streaking toward a land halfway around the world to kill people I had never seen. Nevertheless, I felt relaxed, confident, and determined—oddly at peace. I had long since concluded that North Koreans were the bad guys, their attack on South Korea was unprovoked, they were Communists, and they were a direct threat to Japan and ultimately to America. Actual hatred awaited the discovery of extensive torture and brainwashing of American prisoners.

When the route was identified, we spread our formation, and descended to a few hundred feet above the ground. Almost immediately, and intermittently thereafter, gun flashes blinked below, greeting us at almost every turn. Our presence was obviously radioed ahead, and for some inexplicable reason, I was shocked that people down there were actively engaged in a coordinated effort to kill ME—an otherwise good guy. Such thoughts were short lived for I was twisting and turning at some five hundred knots, spotting a target, and swinging around to attack, only to find it had disappeared into the countryside. It was quickly apparent we had to fire on sight, before they could run for cover, to be effective. We hit a few targets with our cannons, fired our rockets at suspected hiding places, and returned to the *Boxer* unscathed.

There wasn't much to report to the intelligence officer in debriefing, and I doubted I had done much to advance the war effort. But I felt a new surge of self-confidence, almost elation, at having engaged in combat—shooting and being shot at—without flinching. No one can know for sure how he will react until actually tested under fire.

Carrier flight operations, in modern parlance, were "24/7s"—twenty-four hours a day, seven days a week. Thirty-five hundred diverse individuals, all with clearly defined roles, lived, worked, slept, ate, and even played on this powerful fighting ship. As our air group operations and personnel meshed with the ship's company, factions dissolved into teams; and an astonishing intricate and complex bonding occurred. Only about one hundred of us were actually engaged in combat, and all of it occurred out of sight and earshot of the remaining thirty-four hundred men. They had to train, work, and endure all the hardships of being away from their families without the compensating satisfaction of seeing the enemy punished.

I was not unaware of our special roles, even celebrity status for those of us flying jets, but I never witnessed a pilot boast, abuse, or show untoward bravado in the daily routine. There seemed an unspoken but pervading respect for each other's professionalism, and a solid understanding of our mutual dependence. I thought it reflected great credit on the ship's command structure and the navy's organization and training.

Carrier duty was perhaps the ultimate oxymoron—a civilized way to fight a war. We dined in the officer's wardroom on white tablecloths, with heavy silverware and individual cloth napkins and rings. White-jacketed Filipino stewards scurried around to serve us full-course dinners in the evening and assist in providing breakfast and lunch. Early prelaunch breakfasts were served cafeteria style, and featured steak and eggs (high nutrition and low bulk) in preparation for long missions. We usually sat at the same place every day and got to know each other's conversational and eating habits well—in time, often too well.

As a pilot, I had few duties other than flying, which made killing time a major occupation when not in the air. There was always a card game to join or an opponent for chess or Acey Duecy (the navy version of backgammon) in the wardroom. And the small ship's library had plenty of well-used books to read. Evening bull sessions were wide ranging and nonstop, supposedly hewing to the navy's unwritten rule to avoid politics, religion, and women to forestall heated arguments. We hardly talked about anything else.

One particularly stormy evening, I decided to go up on the bridge and see how the situation was being handled. With the ship, my entire universe, violently pitching and rolling, just weaving my way through passageways and up ladders (stairs) was challenging. I envisioned the bridge filled with officers issuing orders, enlisted men scurrying around to execute them, and tension running high. What I found was the officer of the day, a junior officer in his midtwenties, sitting calmly in the captain's chair, surveying the crashing waves through the darkness and driving rain, occasionally glancing at instruments. An enlisted man stood at the giant helm, rhythmically turning it one way and then the other to steady the course. Another enlisted man, "a talker," with earphones and a mike around his neck, stood ready to receive or transmit orders. But none were forthcoming. All systems were working; the course was steady.

With visibility less than a mile, I thought of possible hazards out there as we plunged through the angry ocean in the midst of the vast task force. The large cruiser could misread an order, a destroyer stray off course, an uncharted shoal, or a wayward merchant ship emerge. Yet, everything seemed under control. Of course, the captain was in his quarters a few steps away, and screens and communication channels were manned below, but the officer of the day was in charge. What responsibility and confidence-building for a person so young. Only in the navy!

Midway in the cruise, I was promoted to lieutenant senior grade, and graduated to a small two-man stateroom with comfortable bunks, a wash basin, two combination dresser/desks, and even a small safe for valuables. Lest this appear too cushy, I should add that space was sparse, there were no portholes, and I could still hear engines and catapult shots roaring day and night.

An occasional movie was shown on the hangar deck, the vast area just below the flight deck, where planes were stored, repaired, and moved back and forth on giant elevators. There was even space for a rare basketball game, uniquely challenging because players found themselves running uphill, downhill, and occasionally sideways as the ship pitched and rolled. Baskets were moving targets, sideways and up and down—while the ball was in the air. As a result, scoring was low, but the exercise was good, and it did kill time.

Then there was always the fascination of watching flight operations—sort of a busman's holiday. We congregated on "Vulture's Row," an area high up on the bridge, informally reserved for pilots to observe and perhaps profit from the mistakes of others. It was interesting and occasionally scary to see the landing signal officer symbiotically bringing other pilots into the "groove," signal a cut, and watch them slam down, catch a wire, disengage, and taxi out of the way for the next landing—all in less than a minute. The sound was deafening, timing precise, and teamwork perfect, for the stakes were high. Yet it all seemed routine—until a plane crashed. Over an extended cruise, there were many, and I saw my share of them.

The most spectacular one occurred on a dark night shrouded in mist and low-hanging clouds—the kind that smelled of trouble. The Night Heckler unit was returning from North Korea in their Corsairs, and one got too slow in the groove. The LSO gradually, then vigorously signaled him to increase speed, and receiving little response, frantically waved him off. But it was too late. As the LSO and his assistant dove into their safety net, the Corsair slammed into the edge of the deck with a thunderous metal-against-metal crunch just a few feet away.

Miraculously, the plane hit just aft of the cockpit, splitting it in two, with the front part spinning and screeching up the deck, hitting a barrier, and stopping. What was left of the tail fell back into the churning water. For an instant, silence; then powerful floodlights snapped on, firefighters in asbestos suits and medics poured out of the "Island," and deckhands swarmed over what was left of the plane to rescue the pilot. Fly One's rapid-fire directions crackled over the loudspeakers as we watched, stunned, to see if the pilot, slumped in his seat, had survived. Thankfully, he stirred, then managed a weak wave, and was helped out of the cockpit, shocked but unhurt.

The remains of the Corsair were hoisted by crane forward of the Davis Barrier, a canvas and cable device protecting parked aircraft. The floodlights went out.

Fly One boomed, "CLEAR DECK, RESUME RECOVERY OF AIRCRAFT," and the LSO, a mild-mannered, slight-of-build man (who now seemed ten feet tall), climbed back onto the platform, picked up his paddles, and waved the remaining planes in. It all transpired in less than ten minutes.

There were other crashes with less happy results but the "show" always went on. I remember idly watching a plane enter the landing pattern one afternoon, its wheels lowered and tail hook extended, when suddenly it plunged into the ocean. The plane guard helicopter was over the crash site almost immediately, poised for rescue. But neither the pilot nor any part of the plane surfaced, the sea had simply closed over him. Landing operations, only momentarily interrupted, resumed, and the task force continued on, leaving the helicopter to make one last forlorn circle of the area. The victim, a young ensign, had just joined us as a replacement pilot, and was returning from his first mission. Now he was gone, and few of us even knew his name.

Not all casualties were combatants. The flight deck itself was fraught with danger. The recovery of aircraft was especially daunting, with planes coming in less than a minute apart at over 105 knots to catch a wire with the tail hook and instantly decelerate to zero—actually, less than zero, for the stretched wire pulled the plane slightly backward. A missed wire and the plane either engaged the Davis Barrier, or plowed into parked airplanes on the bow. Missed approaches or delayed wave-offs and planes could wind up in the catwalk. And there was the possibility, though rare, that the arresting wire itself would snap and whip over the deck at lethal speed.

Among the hazards of aircraft launchings was an occasional bad catapult shot, one too weak to provide flying speed, dropping the plane into the path of the carrier. Our operations officer, Tom Chuhak, went in after one such shot and lived to tell about it. He was trapped in his plane, sinking slowly, and with lungs bursting, made one last superhuman effort to break loose. When picked up and returned to the ship, he found he had ripped a tangled parachute strap to get free, a seemingly impossible feat of strength—unless face-to-face with oblivion.

Just starting engines and moving on deck was perilous. There were whirling propellers and flaming tailpipes to avoid, the deafening roar of engine run-ups and catapults to endure, and always, always the oppressive pressure of time. The men guarding the planes and guiding them into position were spread throughout this moving mass of machinery, weaving and signaling, while bracing themselves against a thirty-knot-plus wind over a pitching, rolling deck. One day, having just strapped in and lighted off, I saw the plane captain at my side gasp as if stricken. An instant later, Fly One's voice boomed over the speakers, "STOP ALL ENGINES. STOP ALL ENGINES"—ordering a highly unusual interruption to the launch.

Medical corpsmen rushed out of the Island, past my plane, carrying a stretcher. I was unable to see behind me, but the plane captain shouted that he thought someone had run into a propeller. A few minutes later, the corpsmen came slowly walking back, carrying a blanket-covered, truncated figure on the stretcher. As they passed below me, I could see the top of the victim's head, an outline of his disconnected torso, and most distressing, two legs, feet-first, protruding from the blanket alongside his head. The victim had either jumped or fallen from the wing of a plane and into a whirling propeller. As soon as the corpsmen disappeared in the Island, Fly One, without explanation or comment, gave the order to start engines, and the launch resumed.

Danger even lurked on the hangar deck, where planes were fueled, armed, and serviced. The risk of fire, of course, was always present, but more insidious were the unexpected, unlikely malfunctions of the many intricate instruments of war. One of the worst occurred when a mechanic was leaning into a jet's cockpit, working on an unrelated problem, when the ejection seat inexplicably fired. His injuries were unimaginable, but he was still alive when rushed away by medics. I never learned if he survived.

The routine of daily missions proceeded relentlessly, interrupted only when weather made operations impossible, or the necessary replenishment of fuel, armaments, and other supplies intervened. This too was a perilous exercise requiring special training and superb seamanship. Large supply ships would come alongside, close enough to connect fueling lines and cables over which supplies, and occasionally, people strapped in wildly gyrating "boson's chairs," were transported. It required two massive, heaving and rolling vessels, seldom in sync, to plow through the ocean only yards apart, without hitting each other. It was impressive to watch in calm seas; in rough weather, it was awesome.

Captain Cameron Briggs, the skipper of our carrier, observed the operation from a conspicuous place, stopwatch in hand, issuing orders and comments through a bullhorn. Later, he would inform all hands of the tonnage transported, and the exact amount of time taken compared with previous operations. The stopwatch hanging around his neck became his personal signature, like General Patton's pearl-handled pistols or Ridgeway's live grenade, and he used it to time and record everything that moved.

As one of two carriers in the task force, our air group attacked targets throughout North Korea, concentrating on the eastern area. Our principal missions consisted of armed reconnaissance, photo escorts, flak suppression, and combat air patrols. Assignments for the following day were posted each afternoon in the ready room, and we gathered around to see if our names were on it. If so, we checked the targets assigned, and speculated on risks involved. Although not everyone felt the same way, most seemed disappointed if their name was not listed. I certainly did, and in fact, the more challenging and dangerous the mission, the better I liked it—and I was never quite sure why. Certainly, it reflected the bravado of youth, and I suppose, my inherent tendency to court danger, but underlying it all was a measure of patriotism—the sense of a citizen's duty in a worthy cause. It was a sentiment most of us would have been too embarrassed to express. Surprisingly, though, I never saw anyone display overt hatred of the enemy or undue satisfaction from destroying him.

Among the more hazardous missions was loitering over the front lines, waiting to bomb or strafe targets spotted by controllers on the ground or circling in light planes. Corsairs and Skyraiders were used to loiter; "spotter" pilots flew the light planes, slow, fragile, and unarmed, precluded even from surprise with the constant drone of their engines. I admired but never envied them—more danger by far than I cared to court.

Also vital but unsung was our small contingent of Night Hecklers, who flew Corsairs over enemy territory on most nights—the darker the better. They dropped bombs on suspected targets or routes to disrupt enemy activities, but had no way to judge the results. And then there were the photo pilots in their unarmed jets, swooping in low to take high-resolution pictures of enemy positions, with only one armed fighter escort to protect him or call for help if shot down. On balance, I thought we fighter pilots were the lucky ones.

We operated in all kinds of weather as long as there was sufficient visibility to find assigned routes and see specific targets. Our planes had no radar, no automatic pilots, and few navigational aids, and as described earlier, our gun and rocket sights were little more than illuminated calibration devices projected on the windshield. They provided the framework for judging angles of attack, range, and deflection, but we had to do the judging, while closing on targets at high speed.

Moreover, as previously noted, the airplane itself was the aiming and firing platform, it required immense skill to keep that platform stable at the instant of firing. Turning, pulling Gs, or bouncing in turbulent air inevitably meant missing the target—and most of the targets in North Korea were in turbulent, mountainous areas. Still, our accuracy was quite high, even under the worst conditions, despite the distraction of being targets ourselves during most of the attacks.

Routes with the most traffic, those with railroads, tunnels, and trestles, were generally the most heavily protected. The enemy's weapons of choice were three- and five-inch antiaircraft cannons and the omnipresent "small arms" (rifles and fifty-caliber machine guns). Three-inch shells emitted ominous black puffs of smoke when they exploded, while five-inch shells left white puffs, which always seemed less threatening, though significantly more dangerous. Our defense was speed and intermittent jinking (abruptly changing course and altitude) to evade antiaircraft fire. I often looked back with morbid satisfaction to see puffs from exploding shells tracing the path I had just left. Small arms' fire, on the other hand, was largely invisible, always dangerous, and had to be expected wherever we were.

As the missions piled up, I learned the patterns and practices of the enemy and how to deal with them. Motor transport seldom operated during the day, so I looked for them singly or in pools, generally undercover, hiding until nightfall. Trains ran only at night, and often could be spotted just before dawn, racing for tunnels to hide in, or already in the mouth of tunnels still emitting steam. That left only oxcarts or other makeshift conveyances supplying their front lines during daylight hours. When spotted, the life-or-death question was whether such conveyances were transporting arms and supplies, or merely being used by peasants in the course of eking out a living.

Although our orders to stop everything were unequivocal, most of us, I think, made an effort to decide which was which. At the speeds we flew, there was only a second or two to distinguish soldier from peasant, and war supplies from farm goods—for both would disappear before we could come around for a second pass. The painful dilemma, of course, was whether to hit all of them indiscriminately to provide maximum protection for our troops, or spare those thought to be peasants, and possibly risk the lives of some of those troops if we were wrong. I dealt with it by hitting only people and conveyances that seemed to be part of a pattern even though dispersed, and let those moving singly in isolation to live another day. I did my best to make the distinction in the split-second available, and never second-guessed myself then or in the years since.

Flak suppression missions were a different story. There were no ambiguities about those targets; they had to be important to warrant large-scale attacks by the air group ("Group Gropes"). The mission began by launching waves of bombers well before we were catapulted, at a time calculated to put us over the target just as the bombers arrived. Our job was to go in first, with cannons and rockets blazing, to take out AA fire before the slower, more vulnerable dive bombers attacked. Upon arrival, we circled in echelon formation at around fifteen thousand feet, and peeled off one after the other at three-second intervals into steep dives. This brought us down on the target from every direction ("around the clock"), and into a blizzard of upcoming flak.

I dove as low as I dared before cutting loose with my rockets and cannons. With the enemy's guns pointed almost straight up, and me in a steep dive, we both had low deflection shots, massively increasing our accuracy. "Matching gun barrels," we called it. With flashes from their cannons followed by upcoming tracers and detonating shells clashing with tracers and explosions from my rockets and cannon, it had all the characteristics of a holiday fireworks display except one: there were no sound effects. It was the ultimate test of wills. After several runs, we turned the target over to bombers, returned to the carrier, and as we enjoyed telling them, sipped coffee in the ready room until they landed aboard with their aching butts.

Photo-escort missions were generally less hazardous than "group gropes" and "armed reccos": targets were usually approached from high altitudes to gain surprise and execute a high-speed pass before a meaningful defense could be mustered. Armed with cameras instead of cannons, the photo pilot was completely dependent on his escort for protection. While he was responsible for finding the target and planning the approach, his escort flew above and behind to protect him from possible aerial attack, and spot him for search-and-rescuers if he went down.

The missions were long and lonely, penetrating deep into enemy territory, in total radio silence, constantly scanning empty skies. Only, one day, the sky wasn't empty. I was over the Yalu River, the border between North Korea and China and the farthest point of our mission, when I spotted a MIG fighter coming in, probably from nearby Antung. With an adrenaline rush and pounding pulse at the prospect of my first real dogfight, I turned to intercept him. After a few seconds of closure, he suddenly broke off, swung around, and headed back across the river and safety in the Communist sanctuary.

I was sorely tempted to go after him despite restrictions, but I couldn't leave the unarmed photo pilot unprotected. Even more frustrating was to see the enemy return to his base with planes openly parked along a runway—planes I could have destroyed with one pass, in a matter of seconds, if I didn't mind causing an international incident. I was restrained, of course, by the political decision to contain fighting to the Korean Peninsula even though China had been providing massive supplies and troops to North Korea for months. This was especially frustrating for air force pilots sitting in their F-86s south of the Yalu River, watching as enemy MIGs climbed above them to attack when it was to their advantage—always with the option to return to their sanctuary at will.

CHAPTER 9

MISSION ACCOMPLISHED

O ne day, without warning, the flight schedule was canceled, the *Boxer* veered out of the task force and headed south. No one knew why or could think of a plausible reason, sparking a field day of rumors as we watched the remaining ships sink below the horizon. Suddenly, the veil of mystery was broken by the familiar "NOW HEAR THIS, NOW HEAR THIS" blaring over the ship's loudspeakers, followed by a terse, "This is the captain speaking"— pause—"The USS *Boxer* has been ordered to conduct a brief patrol along the Formosa Straits without escort. We will be sailing in international waters, but within a short distance of Communist China's coast. Although we don't anticipate interference from the Chinese, we should be alert to any activity, and be prepared for any contingency. That is all."

This set off even more rumors, until another voice came over the speakers. "NOW HEAR THIS, NOW HEAR THIS, all VF-721 pilots report immediately to Ready One. I repeat, all VF-721 pilots report immediately to Ready One. That is all." When I arrived, Skipper Woodman was standing in front of the room, impatiently waiting for late arrivals and looking very serious. Without preamble, he led off with, "What I am about to say is highly classified, and it is for your ears only. Under no circumstances should you disclose it to anyone else, and that includes anyone in our air group and on this ship. No one."

He paused for emphasis, and then continued. "Our squadron has been ordered by the highest authority to escort photo planes deep into China, take certain pictures, and get out as quickly as possible. We hope to catch them by surprise, and return to international waters before they react. But if we're unsuccessful, you can expect the Chinese to use all means available to stop us"— pause—"You should also know if anyone goes down, he'll be on his own. No rescue is planned, and the mission will probably be denied."

Then he named four pilots to escort the photo planes, and eight to fly along China's coast to clutter up their radar and fake an incursion farther north so the photos could slip in and out. I was named to the latter group. He then asked those not assigned to leave the room. Now he really had our attention.

The escort pilots were led to another room, where they joined the photo pilots for briefing on specific targets, routes, special codes, and emergency procedures. And we remained to be briefed on our part of the deception. When Woodman, the leader of our flight, briefed us, he included the location of an alternate field in Formosa (Taiwan) in case the *Boxer's* deck got "fouled." One pilot rather naively asked if communications with the tower would be in English or Chinese. Woodman eased the tension by answering with a grin, "I don't know about you, but I plan to speak English."

On mission day, we were up well before dawn, attended to personal preparations and breakfast, reported to the ready room for last-minute briefings, and sat quietly waiting for the order to man planes. Tension was perhaps a tad higher than usual because of the secrecy, not because the mission was any more daunting—at least for those of us providing the smoke screen. We were launched just before dawn, and headed north for the diversion, followed by the photo planes and their escorts, who quickly split off and turned west. Each group carried out its assignment as planned, and was recovered in reverse order without incident. Then the *Boxer* headed north to rejoin the task force, and took up its position as if nothing had occurred. As far as I know, the operation was a success. None of the photo and escort pilots ever talked about it, and none of us ever mentioned it again.

As the number of missions mounted, my familiarity with North Korea expanded, and effectiveness increased. I learned to find my way around mountains and through valleys along major supply routes, and became more knowledgeable about the enemy's favorite hiding places, tactics, and defenses. My ability to spot and hit targets improved dramatically. One of the staples of our strategy was the predawn launch. It began with an early to bed, early to rise (0300) routine of shaving, showering, and the customary steak-and-egg breakfast. Next came donning layers of flight gear (underwear, skintight G-Suit, rubber waterproof immersion suit, life jacket, and a .38 revolver strapped around my waist) and an intelligence briefing, plotting routes, and writing down codes of the day, followed by quiet reflection and waiting. Then, the order crackling over the intercom, "PILOTS, MAN YOUR PLANES. PILOTS, MAN YOUR PLANES." And I would be up on deck, looking for my assigned plane and its captain, in the darkness.

Hunting was best as the first streaks of light filtered through the vanishing night, illuminating an enemy busily delivering supplies to the front. I look for trains racing toward tunnels, and trucks heading for whatever cover they can find. When spotted, they don't have a chance due to my closing speed, firepower, and accuracy. Only occasional AA fire is seen as I emerge silently from the early dawn murk, leaving behind the thunder of a jet engine rolling through the land. A second pass, if required, was something else; AA, seen and unseen, was usually waiting. During the next half hour, a furious fight rages as the sun's rays brighten, the targets dissolve, and the countryside returns to a peaceful, almost bucolic state. Many more flights that day will ensure it stays that way.

On other missions, especially against stationary targets like bridges and staging areas, AA will most certainly be there—sometimes visibly, more often just felt. I pulled up from one attack and heard a sharp metal-on-metal crack behind my cockpit, where highly compressed air and torrents of fuel fed the roaring inferno of the jet engine. Instinctively, I turned toward the beach while checking tailpipe temperature. If it started to rise, fire and explosion would be imminent, and I would have to eject. I stared at the needle for a second or two. It didn't move. A more relaxed check of other systems and controls showed all functioning normally. I radioed Charlie I had been hit, and we headed back to the carrier, where emergency provisions for landing were already underway. None were needed. The bullet, probably from a fifty-caliber machine gun, had miraculously slipped through a ganglion of hoses, fuel lines, jugs, and turbine blades, any one of which could have caused a disaster if severed.

I relived this experience years later, in the movie *The Bridges at Toko-Ri*. The hero, played by William Holden, also a recalled reservist flying a Panther, was hit by small arms' fire while attacking a bridge. Except in the movie, a fuel line was ruptured, spewing fuel into the air, draining his tanks as he headed toward the beach. Sitting in the darkened theater, I felt like screaming at him to throttle up to full power, converting his diminishing fuel to altitude so he could glide beyond the area and perhaps to the beach before his tanks ran dry. Burn it or lose it. Instead, he throttled back to reduce consumption, playing off what little altitude he had left. When his fuel-starved engine shut down, he ditched his plane, and was killed resisting capture. Admittedly, the movie's story line was more dramatic than mine, especially the close up of Frederic March, the task force admiral, being informed of Holden's death and musing mournfully, "Where does America find such men?"

Despite the mounting number of missions and inevitable close calls, I managed to be at peace with danger. It was everywhere and nowhere, and there was no way to avoid it, so I simply decided not to think about it. Even a routine flight off the carrier was hazardous. One day, for example, I was hooked up to the catapult, and the cat officer gave me the one-finger wind up to full power and paused while I made the usual check of my high-pressure pumps. I snapped the throttle back to 50 percent power, and watched the red pump light on my panel blink on for slightly more than two seconds before going off. The backup pump was sluggish but functioning. I was supposed to abort the flight. But if I did, the entire launching sequence would be interrupted, and I would have wasted hours of preparation time. Still at half power, I decided to go anyway, and nodded affirmatively to the cat officer.

To my horror, he gave the signal to launch without waiting for the engine run-up. I jammed the throttle forward, thinking, "You dumb bastard, you were supposed to wait for my salute," but no matter, in the next second or two I would be on my way. But a jet engine takes time to wind up to full power, and I was only at 80 percent when shot off the bow, virtually in a stall, with barely functioning control surfaces. By immediately dipping my nose, playing off the fifty feet or so of height from the deck, and gingerly leveling off just above the water, I managed to stay airborne until enough airspeed was built up to climb out and join my division. Later, the cat officer admitted he had goofed, apologized profusely, and was almost as relieved as I was at the outcome.

Then there was the morning I was scheduled to fly combat air patrol over the fleet, while planes from the air group headed for North Korea. Like most of my squadron mates, I considered flying CAPs to be "milk runs," and tried to avoid them. Carrier doctrine, however, required that at least two jets be launched prior to full carrier operations, and sent up to circle at twenty thousand feet, ready to intercept enemy attacks. When "on station," the pilot checks in with the carrier's combat information center, and remains poised to respond to reports of any incoming unidentified aircraft (a "bogie") picked up by the center's long-range radar.

At that stage of the war, bogies inevitably turned out to be friendly, generally U.S. transports inadvertently wandering near the task force. An intercept consisted of persuading the bogie by radio to change course, or if no response, by sliding in on its wing to enjoy the pilot's expression when he saw a heavily armed fighter signaling to change course. His response was always immediate!

This CAP required an early morning launch, so my plane was already spotted on the catapult, wings folded, fully armed, and ready to go at a moment's notice when I arrived. The plane captain reported favorably on the plane's condition, and I made the usual walk-around inspection, except that with the wings folded I couldn't reach the wingtip tanks to check if they were topped off. No matter, my fuel gauges in the cockpit showed all other tanks full; and everything else checked out, so I had to assume the wingtip tanks were refueled as well. After lighting off, spreading my wings, and making last-minute engine checks, I saluted the cat officer, and the catapult fired.

The plane immediately skewed to the left as it shot along the track, and with tires screeching and smoking, went off the deck slightly sideways. My left wingtip tank was full, but the right one was empty! Despite skewing, the powerful catapult still launched me into the air, but with less speed. As I left the deck, the uneven weight caused my left wing to drop precipitously, and I lacked sufficient speed to pick it up with ailerons. I was headed for a deadly cartwheel into the water, directly in the path of thirty-five thousand tons of steel traveling over thirty knots.

More by instinct than training, I did the only things possible to save me: nose down to pick up a little speed, push right rudder to skid the plane to increase lift on left wing, and play off what little height I had left. It was a replay of the field carrier landing years earlier when the throttle had come off in my hand. Mercifully, the wings leveled just above the water, and I was able to nurse my airspeed along to stay airborne until it could compensate for the empty tank. Meanwhile, I had disappeared over the bow of the carrier, causing horns to blare, flares to fire, and whistles to blow, signaling "Plane Overboard." The carrier had started what would have been a futile emergency turn, when I suddenly reappeared and managed to climb out to my station. But there's more.

I wound around at twenty thousand feet, waiting to respond to intercept requests that never came, while the air group completed its mission, returned, and was recovered. Full tanks and normal fuel conservation measures would have provided sufficient air time to return aboard comfortably. However, with one empty tank, the margin for delay was reduced but acceptable if I stayed at high altitude until cleared to land, and then went straight in. When the last plane was recovered, I was cleared and pushed over at a steep angle to enter the landing pattern as quickly as possible. As I dove through ten thousand feet, my canopy began to frost up; my windshield defroster wasn't functioning properly. At the time, outside temperatures at high altitudes were more than forty degrees below zero, and at sea level, eighty degrees above. The defroster couldn't cope with the spread.

I informed Fly One of the situation, emphasizing my low fuel state, and was cleared for immediate approach. I entered the landing pattern, swiping the windshield with my left hand, trying to get a brief peak at the landing signal officer, quickly returning it to the throttle to fine-tune speed as I approached the carrier. But after each swipe, the windshield immediately frosted again; the already murky view of the LSO dissolved. I took a voluntary wave off, hoping the warm outside air would help clear the frost by the next pass. I received the laconic transmission from the carrier, "Jet 105 cleared for another approach. What state?"—amount of fuel remaining, measured in pounds. I responded, "One-oh-five, roger. Cleared for new approach. State: six hundred"—enough for two more approaches, at best.

I proceeded just far enough upwind to allow for a 180-degree turn and a short downwind leg to set up for the next approach. I kept swiping the windshield, struggling to increase visibility, but making little progress. I was now the only plane in the task force still in the air, with an audience of thousands watching the unfolding drama. Again, I picked up the LSO as I entered the groove, but couldn't see him well enough to make timely responses to his signals. He brought me in as close as he dared, and then waved me off. I went to full power, climbed out of the groove, barely clearing the ramp, and prepared for another—and final—try. "Jet 105 cleared for immediate approach. What state?" "One-oh-five, roger. Commencing immediate approach. State: two fifty"—barely enough for a very tight approach, and if unsuccessful, for a controlled ditching in the ocean.

As if that weren't enough, the task force was heading into a rain squall that had already eclipsed the forward destroyer screen. I would have to execute a nearly-perfect 360-degree turn (minimum upwind and no downwind legs) to save fuel *and* avoid the squall. There was no room for error, no more chances. I had to judge and adjust constantly for the ever-changing relative speeds of airplane, ship, and wind throughout the turn to arrive in the groove at precisely the right altitude, distance, and airspeed to receive a cut.

The windshield had warmed somewhat, requiring fewer swipes, each marginally providing a clearer, longer view of the LSO. He and I both understood it was this pass or never. I arrived in the groove with only enough fuel and visibility for a couple of last-minute signals; I received a cut, dove for the deck, and caught a wire. Not a great landing, but a safe one—so much for the so-called milk run. The sailor who failed to fill the wing tank was removed from duty, demoted, and severely reprimanded. I never met him, and didn't want to.

But there were lighter moments. Like the early morning flight when I decided to skip the mandatory shave, thinking I would be back before most of the senior officers were up. I returned, caught a wire, and expected to taxi forward and return to the sanctity of the ready room when the Air Boss boomed out: "Congratulations, Lt. Rines, you have just made the forty-five thousandth landing on the USS *Boxer*." Oh no! Every carrier made a big deal of a thousandth landing, with a special dinner, big cake, often a skit, and the name of the pilot etched on a permanent plaque. Not bad, but it all started with the captain greeting the pilot as he jumped down from his plane as photographers snapped pictures. Captain Briggs gave me a big broad friendly smile as he shook my hand, but through clenched teeth he was saying, "Why the hell didn't you shave this morning, Lieutenant!"

Operations continued daily, individual missions piled up, and the strain began to show. It was time for a little R and R (rest and recreation) for pilots and crew. The *Boxer* broke off from the task force, and headed for Yokosuka, a large shipping and military port in Japan. The American occupation was still in force, and I braced for a quiet, sullen reception.

Instead, it was a big event and a friendly one. Crowds of people and rows of rickshaws were lined up at the dock, with runners eager to take us wherever we wished to go. They were the ultimate joggers: remarkable speed and endurance, seldom resting, and barely breathing hard. Although they vied aggressively for passengers, I was never comfortable sitting and watching all that human exertion for my benefit. Engine-driven taxis, on the other hand, were sparse, old, and underpowered. We often had to get out and walk up hills to lighten the load, and occasionally found ourselves pushing the taxi on the steeper ones.

We visited Yokohama and Tokyo armed with Japanese script worth 363 yen to the dollar. This made us comparatively rich in that economy, and we lived high for the few days we were there. Drinks cost the equivalent of ten cents, full-course dinners around a dollar, and cameras, typewriters, and Japanese artifacts were extraordinarily inexpensive. We were amazed and a bit suspicious of the outpouring of admiration and goodwill for Americans, their recent conquerors, and their overt desire to please us. Everyone I met, in city or country, old or young, was anxious to tell me how strongly he or she had been against the war, begging the question of why so many fought so long and so hard.

Another cultural puzzler was the dichotomy between their treatment of foreigners and each other. When I asked a traffic policeman for directions one day, he couldn't have been more polite, first by trying to understand my question, and then by helping me find my way. In the midst of our discourse, he spotted a Japanese jaywalker ignoring a traffic light, and stormed after him, shouting and beating him with his club. Then, he returned without comment, and cheerfully went on with his directions. Inscrutable, indeed.

We also spent a few days at a country resort in the foothills of Mount Fuji, reinforcing our newly acquired taste for wealth with grand vistas, excellent food, and an abundance of things to do. It cost us about three dollars a day. We hiked, swam, drank too much, and rested too little. I discovered skis for rent, picked out the best of the lot, a battered wooden pair, and climbed partway up the mountain with a couple of Japanese kids. We skied down a long, open, not particularly steep slope in snow conditions comparable to our spring skiing. It wasn't much of a run, but "skiing Mount Fuji," stirring visions of hair-raising schusses down its treeless side, would be shamelessly dropped by me in the years ahead. We were also exposed to the Japanese custom of coed bathing naked in steaming pools. What they took as a matter of course, sometimes as entire families, we found embarrassing, and strove to maintain our modesty—to their great amusement.

I returned to the task force refreshed if not rested, and found it both strange and exhilarating to climb back into the cockpit and engage once again in the organized chaos of carrier operations. The number of missions resumed climbing: thirty, thirty-five, forty, and still our squadron avoided casualties, though close calls and near misses were everywhere. The other squadrons in the air group were not so fortunate, particularly VF-884 from Olathe, Kansas. It lost close to 50 percent of its pilots, killed in action, missing in action, or from operational losses due to enemy fire, target fixation, mechanical failure, or simply unknown causes.

We seldom mingled with pilots from the other squadrons except at mealtimes, so I knew few of them personally. However, as their losses grew, some were nearby table companions in the fixed seating arrangement at dinner. One night, the person seated on my right failed to arrive, and I learned he was shot down and presumed lost. Not long after, the person seated next to the person on my left was killed, and weeks later the one seated directly across from me was gone. I felt badly for them and their families, of course, but somehow was not shaken or upset, and never fully understood why.

Undoubtedly, part of the reason was the armor of indestructibility possessed by the young, and part was self-confidence reinforced by training. But I think, mostly it was the transitory nature of service relationships during wartime. Good friends were always being transferred to other duties and not seen again, and so, in a sense, death was like a permanent transfer without good-bye. Then, too, there were none of the customary trappings for the deceased—no funeral services, grieving relatives, or ceremonies, not even a commemorative moment of silence. Nothing. Just the assignment of a fellow pilot to go through the dead man's personal effects to avoid sending anything embarrassing to his next of kin. I saw only one overt reaction that still stays with me: a lone pilot slowly sifting through a friend's personal effects, crying. Otherwise, life went on as before.

This insensitivity wasn't only around combat, for I recall a similar instance of callousness on a long-forgotten dive-bombing training flight some twenty miles off the Florida West Coast. I was at ten thousand feet, watching a friend peel off into a steep descent for a low-level drop of a dye canister to be used as a target. He flew lower and lower, and suddenly I saw a large splash. Someone radioed, "Did he go in?" I responded, "It looked like it. I'll go down and see." I dove down in a tight spiral to find only dye marker slowly spreading on the water. I reported this to the flight leader, who immediately called air/sea rescue, and a helicopter was dispatched. By the time it arrived, there was little left to see or do—no pilot, no debris, just that slowly dissolving orange stain. We flew back, filed an accident report, and I went ahead with a planned double date that the deceased and I had planned for the evening, explaining that my friend couldn't make it and why. The girls didn't know whether to believe me or not. No wonder. I'm appalled to think that I could be so unfeeling. But it was just the way it was.

Our tour of duty was more than half over. We had become true veterans, concentrating on the tasks at hand, only mildly aware of the politics of war at home. So we were surprised and shocked one morning to read that General MacArthur had been relieved of his command. It developed that his relentless pressure on the Truman administration to allow us to hit the enemy beyond North Korea's boundaries had gone too far. He had argued correctly that the sanctuary from which Chinese "volunteers" and supplies were pouring over the border was costing countless American lives. On the other hand, the administration believed that attacking across the border might escalate the conflict, perhaps leading to a ground war on Chinese soil—a risk they understandably wanted to avoid.

To those of us fighting the war, however, the argument seemed little more than finely drawn debating points because our forces were already in combat with hundreds of thousands of Chinese "volunteers" who had poured across the border without warning in the deadly Chosen Reservoir battles, and their troops, and planes were continuing to stream into North Korea. Today, some fifty years later, the issue is but a minor historical footnote to the war, an academic debate without partisans or adversaries. The world has moved on, leaving uncounted souls lying in the dust.

A new command was installed, led by General Ridgeway, and the ground war stabilized along the Thirty-eighth Parallel, the original demarcation line between North and South before North Korea's invasion. In the following months, many battles were fought and lives lost in that difficult, mountainous terrain, with few meaningful results. From the air, the forces were distinguishable by bustling activity in the South, and virtually none in the North where an estimated five hundred thousand North Korean and Chinese troops were arrayed against us. Only brightly colored panels denoting friendly forces showed us the twisting, undulating front lines. The enemy launched several large-scale offensives in an effort to break through, but all were thrown back with heavy casualties. That left sporadic attacks to gain tactical positions on hills with numbers instead of names, except for one, the infamous Pork Chop Hill, a killing ground that kept changing hands.

Then one day it was announced that North Korea had agreed to begin negotiations for a ceasefire. The news caused great excitement aboard ship and sparked a small celebration for the end of the war now seemed imminent. But agreement proved impossible on even the smallest details (like the shape of the conference table), to say nothing about geographic decisions, prisoner exchanges, lines of withdrawal, and so on. Neither side had the heart or incentive to launch large offensives, but the air war continued apace.

Most of the larger cities such as Hungnam and Hamhung in the northeastern part of the country had been reduced to rubble, though we continued to fly armed reccos on the supply routes in that area. I was appalled to see the terrible terrain around the Chosen Reservoir, and thought of the horror shared by young marines of suddenly hearing bugles on a pitch-black night and finding the surrounding hills alive with Chinese troops. The story of how the marines extricated themselves, "advancing to the rear," in freezing weather, often in hand-to-hand combat, leaving no dead behind, is an American classic, and surely depicts one of the corps' finest hours.

We continued to interdict those routes, but most of our work was closer to the front lines. I was hit again when rolling into an attack on a concentration of enemy trucks and supplies. A blue flash, a loud bang, and a small air bump, and

I knew that this time it was a much larger shell, at least a three-incher. I immediately pulled up and turned toward the beach while assessing the damage. It had penetrated just in front of the canopy, where there was little danger of fire, so my first concern was the effect it might have on my system controls. Again, I was lucky. My hydraulic and electrical systems were functioning normally, and I had only lost radio communications, a situation I could deal with. I turned back and joined up on a member of my flight and through hand signals conveyed my situation and desire to return to the *Boxer*. He led the way and radioed ahead, requesting priority clearance.

By the time we arrived, the carrier deck was alive with emergency equipment and personnel ready to assist. I made a routine landing, and was swarmed over by deckhands checking the damage and potential hazard from my own guns and ammunition in the nose section. I clambered out of the cockpit, examined a large hole and the path the shell followed, and couldn't help thinking that if the gunner had fired a nanosecond later—but I didn't dwell on it.

Our departure date for going home was getting closer as the number and variety of missions flown kept climbing. I had been awarded two Air Medals, each for flying twenty missions in which at least one involved enough heroics to merit the citations. Sixty missions were generally required to qualify for a Distinguished Flying Cross, provided one or more of those missions were deemed sufficiently noteworthy. That was not difficult to do given the nature of our work.

I wound up with a total of fifty-five missions, within shouting distance of a DFC, as did most of my squadron mates, but I doubt any of us was particularly disappointed by failing to reach the magic number. Not that the pat on the back that medals symbolized wasn't appreciated, it just didn't mean much in our lives then, or later. There were no award ceremonies, only a brief comment and certifying letter when they were handed out, and one more ribbon to pin on our uniforms. Mine, like most, have lain buried in an attic trunk for the past half century.

The day finally arrived, largely unheralded, when the *Boxer* officially left station and headed home. Flight operations ceased, and our daily routine became little more than an exercise in killing time. There was no structure, no schedule, nothing new to read or say, just a passive, languorous tracking of the ship's progress through the endless ocean. But gradually, a feeling of pleasure, even pride, grew as the prospect of going home approached.

We had acquitted ourselves well in a worthwhile mission, blunting the virulent Communism of Kim Il Sung in North Korea, Mao Zedong in China, and Joseph Stalin in the Soviet Union, and preserving the freedom of the South Korean people. Subsequent events on the divided peninsula showcased the failure of Communism for all the world to see as North Korea remained mired in poverty and a continuing threat to world peace, while South Korea became an industrial powerhouse and an important part of the region's defense. The war finally ended in July 1953. More than 36,000 Americans had lost their lives.

Everything changed as we neared the California coast. Planning, packing, and pulse rates quickened as the countdown to arrival continued. Off-loading a carrier was almost as complicated as loading one, and clipboards blossomed once again as inventories were counted, dispositions were decided, and plans and schedules were coordinated. It hardly needs stating that married men were given the earliest opportunity to leave the ship, and we bachelors took responsibility for the heavy lifting. The pilots selected to fly our planes off the carrier to San Diego were the big prize winners for they would arrive before the ship docked. We all shared their excitement as they mounted their planes, taxied forward, and catapulted off the deck for the last time, glorying in the fact that they would not return—a fitting metaphor for Mission Accomplished.

Finally, I too found myself with a clipboard, a large crew, an assignment of trucks, and only a vague idea of what to do with them. Finding out and doing it kept me too busy to envy the excitement of families being reunited while mine was three thousand miles away. I was even too busy to get to a phone and call home that first day as I coped with the chaotic process of unloading and stowing the squadron's belongings. Early the next day, I received a call from Ike Morrison, my boyhood chum in Berlin, who somehow figured out how to reach me. After asking if I was all right, he said, "You should call your mother right away. She is sick with worry because she hasn't heard from you." I was dumbstruck and embarrassed for not calling her. It hadn't occurred to me that she would know the exact day of my arrival in California.

I dropped everything to get to an outside phone, and will never forget the relief, joy, love, and pure excitement in her voice when she answered. I had failed to appreciate how much my parents worried—the sleepless nights, awful dreams, and constant fear of answering the doorbell to find a somber naval officer standing there. The armor of invincibility of the young can never be adequately understood by the old—as I was to learn firsthand when my own kids were growing up.

I received two weeks' leave, and returned home a much more mature person than the one who left in a flurry of telegrams two and a half years earlier. For the returning Korean veterans, homecoming was essentially a nonevent. There were no backslapping reunions of old pals, no speeches, and no parades for there was no clear ending. The war just petered out as the negotiated peace moved glacially to conclusion, and the veterans filtered back to the States, unheralded.

Berlin seemed smaller and more confining than ever, and the thought of a career in optometry was even more unattractive and remote. But it was not yet decision time, as I was still on active duty for an indeterminate period and had to report back to the squadron. I returned by way of Chicago, where I bought my first new car, a 1950 Chevrolet convertible, to drive back to NAS Miramar, our new base just outside of San Diego. The squadron was reconstituted, and a change of command brought in a new skipper to replace Woodman, who had gained our fervent respect for leading us unscathed through the Korean campaign. Those happy odds caught up with VF-721 on its next tour, however. Five pilots (almost 20 percent) were lost.

As we awaited assignment to other duties, I flew enough to stay current, helped integrate replacements, and pass on what I had learned in combat. And, of course, there were weekends in Palm Springs.

CHAPTER 10

HOLLYWOOD

I ronically, our reception in Palm Springs was probably the closest we came to a real homecoming from the Korean War. It seemed we had actually been missed, and some of our friends even appeared interested in what had gone on over there. They were, to be sure, mostly innkeepers and bartenders, and of course, the doorman at the Racquet Club. But they also included citizens and patrons we had come to know and like. Dinah Shore, for example, gave a cocktail reception in our honor for no other reason than to show her appreciation for our service to country. Grace Pope was as kind and hospitable as ever, so it was nice to be back.

We were having a drink at the Doll House, a favorite Palm Springs nightclub, when a party of five arrived: two couples and one most attractive young woman. In due course, I managed to introduce myself to her and ask her to dance. I learned her name was Helen Koford, she lived in Glendale with her parents, and she was a Mormon, but not much else. We got on very well together, and by the time they were ready to leave, I had her phone number and an agreement to meet again.

As I said good night to her friends, one of them congratulated me for "picking up a movie star" and told me Helen's screen name was Terry Moore. I failed to be impressed since I had never seen or heard of the actress, but it turned out just about everyone else had. She was, as I soon learned, a rising Hollywood star as well as that lovely young person with a sparkling personality I had spent the evening with, and whose life, it turned out, was more complicated than first appeared.

When I called a week or so later, she wanted me to know that she was married but separated from (and in the process of divorcing) Glenn Davis, the former West Point all-American football player. That was all right with me, but on our first date she mentioned she was also seeing Howard Hughes, the billionaire movie mogul and owner of TWA Airlines. On several later dates, I was asked to drop her off at a prearranged nearby street corner, where her mother would be waiting in a car to drive her home. This clandestine arrangement, I was told, had to do with her ongoing divorce proceedings with Davis, but later press reports suggested the practice had more to do with Hughes's penchant for keeping a close eye on his girlfriends.

No matter, Terry and I spent time together in both Los Angeles and San Diego (where I was still stationed), and along with her charms, I came to enjoy the reflected glow from her celebrity status, and of course, the challenge of competing with Hughes. She talked freely about him and his activities, and especially her effort to persuade him to create a medical research foundation with some of his millions. Terry—and undoubtedly others—succeeded, and the Howard Hughes Medical Institute was officially founded in 1953. Alive and well today, it is annually contributing millions of dollars for research, advancing the health of the nation and the world.

Hughes was at the peak of his illustrious career, and as a billionaire and owner of RKO studios was most attractive to women in Hollywood, where he could make or break careers. Although I cavalierly dismissed him as a "professional bachelor," I rather admired his iconic style, and certainly was impressed by his flying exploits. Our competitive pas de deux got a bit unbalanced at times, like the weekend I took her for a drive in the country in my Chevrolet convertible on Saturday, and he took her up alone in a four-engine Constellation on Sunday. But I managed.

My status in the squadron was dramatically enhanced when Terry accepted an invitation to one of our parties at the officer's club in Miramar. She dazzled the pilots, of course, and mingled easily with their wives, one of whom had shared a mirror with her in the ladies' room before being introduced and told her she "looked just like Terry Moore." Terry had responded quietly, "I am Terry Moore," but was unable to convince her until they found themselves at the same party.

Terry was fascinated with flying and well on her way to earning a pilot's license, so the next morning I took her down to the flight line and let her sit in the cockpit of an F9F Panther. I pointed out rocket and cannon firing mechanisms, showed her how to manipulate the flight controls, "read" the instrument panel, and described some of the sensations of flight in a high-speed jet.

She was suitably impressed, so much so that somehow the experience made its way into one of the popular movie magazines—only it had her actually flying with me in the jet and experiencing the stresses and sensations firsthand. Alas, not true, but I didn't mind as long as the story escaped the attention of navy brass, because, at least for the moment, it put me one up on Hughes and his propeller-driven Constellation.

Her career was soaring, aided by recent roles in several widely acclaimed movies, one of which, *Come Back, Little Sheba*, put her in contention for an Academy Award nomination for best supporting actress. We occasionally went to her movies in local theaters; and I would receive a running account of the happenings behind the camera, as well as tricks of the trade in front of it, like maneuvering a more favorable camera angle, or upstaging scenes with subtle mannerisms without alerting the director.

After one movie, we were sitting in the living room of her parents' home when she produced a script she was working on and asked me to read the starring role opposite her. I demurred for I had never acted, even in a school play, and had little interest in theatrics. She persisted, so I read, probably in a monotone, and certainly without enthusiasm as we played out a dramatic scene. She, on the other hand, displayed an astonishing range of emotions with consummate ease. I was not a great costar. Whatever her purpose or however subtle the test, it was clear I had not passed. I was, if anything, relieved.

It was all great fun. She was beautiful and vivacious, and we had developed a wonderful, easy relationship; one that, at least on my part, was getting serious. Then George Oden, a fellow instrument instructor and close friend, and I received orders to proceed immediately to NAS Alameda, across the bay from San Francisco, to create a jet instrument-training facility for fleet pilots. I called Terry to break the news. We agreed to see each other often anyway, and I headed north to join an instrument-training unit, flying twin-engine Beachcraft, while awaiting arrival of TV-2s, the navy's first two-seater jet.

When George and I arrived, the instructors were still teaching the same old instrument-flying techniques, and following procedures and protocols used for flight on domestic airways. We had no choice but to continue that program until the jets arrived, but tried to relate the training to fleet operations whenever possible. It was a real comedown for me to wind around San Francisco Bay, six thousand feet or lower, at the excruciatingly slow speed of 160 knots. However, it did sharpen my own instrument-flying skills, and enhanced my instructing techniques, demonstrating once again that teaching is an effective way to learn.

When the jets finally arrived, we embarked on an accelerated effort to check out the other instructors, many of whom hadn't flown a single-engine plane since their cadet days. It was hair-raising to sit in the backseat, with limited visibility, trying to demonstrate and coach seasoned, often hide-bound multiengine pilots how to fly a jet. Landings were especially daunting, and I often wound up gently riding the controls—for his welfare as well as mine.

It was also satisfying and certainly ego-building to bring them along, while developing new techniques and protocols for incoming fleet students. I couldn't have been more enthused or more immersed in the project. Terry and I continued our relationship by mail, phone, and occasional weekend visits, but eventually we succumbed to the perils of distance and our respective all-consuming activities, and drifted apart.

One of my students was a full commander, high on the staff of the Pacific Fleet headquarters to which our unit reported. He had had several tours of sea duty to his credit and many hours in the air, but all of them in conventional aircraft. We liked each other immediately, flew well together, and he requested that he only be scheduled with me. A quick study, an accomplished pilot, and a commanding presence, he sailed through the syllabus and continued flying with me whenever he could, building his proficiency. When time for my release from the navy approached, he took me aside one day and asked if I would extend for a year to design a totally new ground and flight instrument-training program for jets, oriented specifically for fleet pilots. I saw it as a chance to play a key role on the cutting edge of naval aviation, and seized it.

One of the first challenges Oden and I faced was how to mesh our operations with commercial air traffic in the Bay area, especially during high-density traffic in bad weather—which was often. Because of the jet's higher speeds and limited endurance, we couldn't circle in conventional holding patterns, stacked in thousand-foot separations, waiting to land. And, of course, new departure patterns had to be developed to allow high speed, fast-climbing jets to join airways crowded with slower propeller-driven aircraft. We worked on the problem and tried many solutions, until we finally put together one that seemed to work without disrupting normal commercial traffic. We arranged a visit to the air-traffic control center to test our ideas and see if it would work for them. Although I had interacted with approach controls for years as a pilot, I had never actually seen a center in operation.

It was not impressive. There were banks of controllers sitting before radar screens, each with responsibility for several planes represented by small oblong wooden slats. These were stacked in slots on a board in front of the controller in the order received. He would work each plane through his area, and then turn it over to the next controller by tossing the slat to him—a casual way to treat a proxy for a plane-load of passengers and crew. The atmosphere was quite relaxed, with little of the tension generally ascribed to the job, although bad weather and emergencies undoubtedly elevated it. As a pilot, the visit reinforced my skepticism of early "controller burnout" claims because however critical a situation was, their lives were never at risk, unlike that of the pilots they were controlling. And "burnout" was never part of our lexicon.

To avoid stacking and interfering with civilian traffic, we devised a system to bring jets in at twenty thousand feet to an airway's "outer marker" (signaled by a blinking red light on our instrument panel) to begin the approach. Located twenty-four miles from the airport radio station, the pilot was cleared immediately to chop power, lower flaps and landing gear, and push over to descend at four thousand feet per minute, then level off at ten thousand to cross the inner marker (twelve miles from the station). At that point, he resumed his descent to cross the radio station at a specified altitude for an approach to the assigned runway. This procedure allowed conventional aircraft to stack up to nine thousand feet at the inner marker, and as necessary, to higher altitudes at the outer marker, while jets were coming in over them for priority landings.

For departures, we designed specific headings after takeoff for an off-airway penetration to twenty thousand feet before joining the airway and proceeding on course. The CAA (since named FAA) controllers listened to our proposals, and though dubious, were willing to try them. We flew several approaches in clear weather under their control to test and smooth out procedures, and then a few more under actual instrument conditions. It proved to be a simple low-tech system that worked, and became standard procedure for the area, until commercial jets arrived and more sophisticated navigational equipment was deployed.

After setting up that program and training the instructors, Oden and I were transferred to NAS Moffett Field in Palo Alto, specifically to train fighter squadrons prior to shipping out to the fleet. These were my kind of guys, well trained, enthusiastic, and anxious to learn. I decided to create a wholly new training syllabus rather than merely modifying conventional procedures. Not only approaches and departures from airports needed redesigning but even standard cross-country flight on major airways had to be reconfigured. For the first time, with newly installed radio direction finders, we were able to fly point to point with little concern for other traffic at our high altitudes, saving time and fuel, while relieving airway congestion.

I wrote an entirely new ground-school program, incorporating new procedures and recasting many of the domestic flight rules to accord with the realities of actual fleet operations, and using my recent combat experience, to relate them to actual situations. I also worked out new flight patterns, instrument-scanning techniques, and procedures for ground-controlled approaches and instrument takeoffs. And I spent time learning how each of the flight instruments worked technically to understand better their limitations and possible malfunctions, and how to deal with them. Then I put it all together, flight by flight and hour by hour, into a ground-school manual and flight schedule that each student pilot had to complete. None of this was "rocket science," but it produced the kind of program pilots needed, and one I wish I had had before shipping out. I like to think some lives were saved and more missions were accomplished because of our work.

As always, it was in actual flight that students really learned, and I spent hundreds of hours in the backseat, remonstrating, praising, and grading them on their performance. By this time, both Oden and I had earned "Green Cards," the highest instrument certification conferred, qualifying us to fly all types of aircraft in all-weather conditions, and the authority to clear ourselves below "minimums" in certain circumstances. Working with experienced pilots as students, we were able take them to the high level of skill and confidence necessary for truly all-weather flight operations.

Landing on instruments in a single-engine jet was especially difficult because the pilot had to do everything—fly, navigate, and communicate—alone. The navy employed the Ground Controlled Approach (GCA) system that required coordinated interaction with a controller sitting before a radar screen in a trailer next to the duty runway, calling for minute heading and altitude changes to keep the incoming plane on "glide path." The lower the pilot gets, the more critical the changes, until he finally breaks out a few hundred feet from the runway. Then he has to make the critical transition to visual flight, leaving a world of moving dials and needles to recapture reality, in a matter of seconds. It was challenging but crucial that sitting in the backseat I let the student fly the approach without interference. The old adage "Students learn by their mistakes" was not easy to apply when even the smallest one could be fatal.

Then there was the need for retooling the student's ability to recover from "unusual attitudes." This drew on the same knowledge and techniques learned as cadets in the old Vibrator, but now they were far more difficult to manage due to faster speeds, higher altitudes, and more punishing Gs. I constantly pounded into them the need "to stay cool, study the instruments, figure out what's happening, and then—and only then—take action to regain straight and level flight." Easy enough to say, but difficult to do when confused, disoriented, and probably scared in actual storm conditions. I tried to put my students into enough difficult situations (inverted, going straight up or down) often enough to make successful recoveries almost routine. And that built real confidence.

In the midst of all this, the Bureau of Naval Personnel in Washington, typically without notice, ordered me to report to the training command at Pensacola for instructor duty. When I showed the commander my orders, he said, in no uncertain terms, "Don't worry about it. You're staying here." His power obviously went beyond rank for within the week, I received new orders officially canceling the first ones, signed by an officer ranking considerably higher than the originator of the transfer. I was grateful and suitably impressed, so one day, when he casually asked if I would be interested in becoming a Blue Angel, I took the query seriously. My spirits soared. I was the right age, single, and certainly had the necessary flight qualifications, including recent combat experience. I loved flying, and there was no more glamorous or challenging way to do it. I could almost taste it.

Then reality intruded. The training and performance schedules would require a commitment of at least five years, probably more, and possibly a transfer to the regular navy from the reserves. Unless I wanted to make the navy a career, which I had already decided against, I had to get back to civilian life and start making up for lost time. I wrestled with the possibility for a few days, and then reluctantly declined. I have never regretted the decision; it was simply assigned to the "you can't do everything" file.

I flew at least two or three training flights a day; a consuming schedule that happily didn't obviate time for play. There were girls to date and parties to go to, and 100 percent oxygen available for morning-after hangovers. I loved San Francisco, and took full advantage of its culture and nightlife. Among highlights at the time were Louie Armstrong and Ella Fitzgerald performing together at the intimate Hangover Club, frenetic Hawaiian dancing in the Tonga Room at the Fairmont Hotel, various jazz clubs, and superb dining in Chinatown and Fisherman's Wharf before the tourists took over.

A friend of mine bought a small used sailboat, which we sanded and painted weekends in Sasaulito, a small town just north of the Golden Gate Bridge, and eventually spent many happy hours sailing in the vast San Francisco Bay. I learned to handle the unpredictable winds and play them off against rushing tides—a fitting introduction to a sport that would become a lifelong interest. I reveled in San Francisco's moderate winter, especially on weekends when I could put my convertible top down, stash skis in the backseat, and drive to within thirty miles of deep powder skiing high in the Sierra Mountains, before putting it back up.

On other weekends, I invited bachelor friends to join me on flights to Las Vegas and Palm Springs. As an instructor, I was encouraged to fly on my own time to maintain proficiency. I needed only to flick a switch on my office intercom to order up a jet or a twin-engine Beechcraft gassed and ready to go. I usually lined up three or four fellow officers to take off for Las Vegas after work on Friday. We would check into a large, expensive suite in the fanciest hotel in town (cheap when divided among us), gambled, took in the best shows, caroused, and returned Sunday night. To limit financial exposure, we each took a small amount of cash to gamble, and pledged solemnly not to lend to one another. This was sorely tested one Friday night when I got cleaned before dinner, and spent a very long weekend pleading for replenishments—to no avail. They enjoyed reminding me it was my rule.

One day, out of the blue, I was invited to a small midweek dinner party at the Red Roof Ranch, a posh private home in Palm Springs. I initially declined because of the distance and my heavy flight schedule; but the hostess, a friend of the inestimable Mrs. Pope, persisted, pointing out that the guest list included, among others, Doris Duke, one of William Randolph Hearst's sons, and Bill Lear, builder of the famed Lear Jet. It sounded too intriguing to pass up, especially the opportunity to meet Lear, an icon in aviation, so I accepted and went to work on the logistics.

Getting there was no problem for I could fly down after my last scheduled flight, and at five hundred knots, make it to Palm Springs in time for dinner. They promised to have a car waiting for me at the airport. There would be no jet fuel available; but if I topped off my tanks before leaving and flew at high altitude, I could make it down and back. The difficult part was getting off early enough the next morning to return in time for my first scheduled flight.

Then there was the question of landing and taking off at the small Palm Springs airport. It was not equipped to handle jets, probably one had never landed there; and the primary runway was barely long enough for my plane to make it off the ground. That left the difficult question of getting the engine started. Although it was possible to crank it up once on the battery, we always used an auxiliary starting unit, which the airport would not have. I just had to hope the plane's emergency battery would be strong enough to light off the engine on first try. Failure to start would create a situation too embarrassing to contemplate. So I didn't.

The flight down and the pickup at the airport worked well. The "ranch" had little land but many interconnected stand-alone structures for living, dining, and sleeping, all set among exotic plantings and grouped around a large swimming pool. I joined the other dozen or so guests for cocktails by the pool, followed by a leisurely stroll along canopied paths to the dining room, and an elaborate dinner, gracefully served, spiced with spirited conversation. Then it was on to the "library," another stand-alone structure, for nightcaps. Although easily the youngest (and certainly the poorest) among them, I was comfortable and mildly intrigued by the conversational and social interplay at their level. Doris Duke, for example, was ordinary in conversation but quite extraordinary in appearance: long black dress, jet-black hair, and noticeably slanted eyes (facelift?) that peered from a pale, almost white face.

With her was a much younger man named Joe Castro, a hip piano player from a Chicago nightclub; she enjoyed his playing so much she took him with her. He cheerfully accepted his kept role, and hugely enjoyed the many perks that went with it. Duke, apparently impressed with the jazz scene, alternated "jive talk" with him and otherwise normal conversation with the rest of us. They were headed for Hawaii later that week.

Lear was engulfed in a telephone conference call and never appeared, so I never met him. The others were interested in learning what jet flight was like, how the Korean War was progressing, and whether the peace talks were going anywhere. As the evening wound down, we were sitting around, swapping stories, when one prominent guest led into one of his with the surprising phrase "I had a wife once who . . ." Surprised at this segue phrasing, I quickly looked at his attractive young wife sitting across from me. With a smile, she held up four fingers, and mouthed quietly, "I'm number four."

And so it went. But time was running on, so I reluctantly bid them good night, citing my early dawn takeoff. It was still dark when the driver dropped me off at the airport the next morning, and thankfully, no one was around, even in the control tower. I headed directly to my plane, and after a quick walk-around inspection, got settled into the cockpit. I flicked on the required switches, held my breath, and started cranking up the engine. At first reluctantly and then more easily, the compressor fans accelerated (as the batteries were draining) to reach that magical speed, when I turned on the fuel and hit the igniter switch. There was a momentary delay, then the beautiful sound of a jet engine winding up to a steady whine, as I watched the tailpipe temperature gauge rise rapidly and then stabilize.

I taxied to the end of the runway, using minimum power to be as quiet as possible, for as long as I could. The sun was just peeping over the horizon, and most of the townsmen were still asleep, blissfully unaware of the thunderous greeting awaiting them. With a silent apology, I pushed the throttle full forward, roared down the runway, lifting off with little room to spare. I stayed at treetop level until I disappeared over the horizon, and the reverberations dissipated. The shock effect on the citizenry surely took a little longer. I arrived back at Moffitt Field in time for my first student flight, and went back to work.

Heading back to base from my last flight one day, I watched as my student, still under the hood, veered off course. Glancing at my instruments, it was clear he was relying on the radio direction finder homing in on the base and not cross checking with his compass as he should. Most of the time it wouldn't have made much difference, but that day there happened to be an unusually strong storm system over the Sierra Mountains, and its static was pulling the directional needle toward the system, and he was blithely following it. It had been a long day of flying, my backside hurt, and I was anxious to get back for a shower and drink before dinner. But the opportunity to teach a lasting lesson was too good to pass up, so I let him continue.

Believing he was on the correct course, he started his descent and painstakingly followed the static-distorted direction finder into the mountain range. I let him go as low as I dared, and then said, "I've got it, pop the hood." When he looked up, we were face to face with a towering peak. I jammed on full power and made a tight climbing turn to safety, letting him digest the fact that in a real-flight situation, he would now be dead, one more victim of an unexplained accident. He was understandably subdued on the way back to the field, and I chose not to lecture him. I wanted to let the experience sink in. On the ground, he limited his remarks to a laconic, "Thanks, I learned a lesson today." Nothing more needed to be said.

As a naval officer, I was required to take my turn as security Officer of the Day for the entire naval air station. Among other duties, I had to make sure that the prescribed guards were at their posts, deal with personnel problems, and sleep in the hangar security office to be readily available for any contingencies. Nothing of great import ever occurred, so I was startled to be awakened and informed that I had a long-distance call from someone who insisted on being put through. I picked up the phone and heard my brother Lloyd say quietly, without preamble, "Chobe, I have some bad news. Dad died tonight." Only half-awake and dazed, I arranged for relief from security duty, returned to my quarters, and put in for an emergency leave. A newly arrived former squadron mate, Bob Roseberry, drove me to the airport, and I flew out later that morning.

When I arrived home, I learned that my father's remaining kidney had suddenly failed, and there had been no way to save him. Kidney dialysis had not yet been developed. He was just sixty-four years old, only one year from retirement.

Services were scheduled in our Baptist church, and custom dictated that they be conducted with an open casket, preceded by visiting hours in a funeral home on afternoons and evenings, where family members received condolences. The custom did little to soften pain or provide time for reflection, but like the traditional Irish wake, it served to distract and defer deeper feelings of grief. The last evening, I lingered alone with him after the obligatory hours of viewing were over. Looking down at that strong man in repose, at the hands that had held me, and the face that had crinkled in smiles so often, I thought of how hard he had worked, how much he'd accomplished, his devotion to family, and the esteem he had earned among peers. Through the tears, I concluded that here, in the context of his life, lay a truly successful man, and vowed that in my life I would try to do as well. I am still trying.

I stayed with my mother for a few days to help console her and deal with our loss, but my older brother, sister-in-law, and sister still lived in Berlin and provided the primary emotional support. Mother was strong, as always, but the pain was intense and lasting, reflecting the strength and joys of their long marriage. Then I returned to Moffitt Field to resume the heavy training schedule and pick up my life.

But somehow it seemed different. I didn't feel the same gusto to take off in the morning, inspire students, and "push the envelope" in flight. The syllabus had been shaped and honed, new instructors had arrived and been trained, and the program's success amply confirmed by reports from the fleet. My pioneering days seemed over. And life in San Francisco had also lost its newness and some of its excitement, and I became aware of a faint tug from the East Coast. It was time to move on, either to another challenge in aviation or return to civilian life.

Oden felt the same way, and was seriously thinking of flying commercially. In fact, he had already scheduled an interview with American Airlines and asked me to accompany him. I agreed, but only to learn more about the job, not because of real interest. The interview was short and to the point. There was a shortage of trained pilots at the time, and American offered to hire us on the spot. Despite the glamour still associated with flying and an attractive starting salary, I was put off by a career that was so dependent on union seniority for promotion and increased pay, and where the flying was likely to be considerably less challenging. I turned the airline down as did Oden, at least partly because of my attitude. He changed his mind about a year later, joined American, and spent his entire career with the airline. He liked to remind me that his seniority and hence his promotion to captain was long delayed because so many pilots were hired in the meantime—and it was my fault.

I now seriously began thinking about life after the navy. By this time, optometry was out; a career in airline management was a possibility, and faint stirrings of interest in the investment business arose when I sought ways to invest my cash savings accumulated on sea duty. Oden remembers the day I asked him to "tell me all about the investment business" over lunch one day. As a business graduate of Northwestern University and a CPA, he was able to provide a broad outline of the business. I was to spend the next forty years filling it in.

Shortly thereafter, one of my instructors left the navy to work for a small brokerage firm in San Francisco, and suggested I might want to join him. He arranged an interview with the president of the company, and I was offered a job, subject to my release from the navy. While thinking about it, I unexpectedly received orders to report to the Bureau of Aeronautics in Washington! I had earlier made known my desire to be a test pilot for the bureau's Office of Naval Research, and presumed it had come through. I put civilian career plans on hold, hurriedly packed, sold my Chevrolet, and hitched a ride on a navy torpedo bomber to Lansing, Michigan, to pick up an Oldsmobile convertible at the factory. Then it was off to Washington in high spirits and great expectations.

Part 4

MARRIAGE AND A NEW CAREER

Although the end of the war in Korea had yet to be declared, and fighting was still going on, it seldom was page-one news. That chapter in my life was essentially over; I was ready to return to civilian life. Only the abrupt receipt of orders and the lure of yet another challenge in flight, this time with the Office of Naval Research, could hold my interest. So I was anxious to report to the Bureau of Aeronautics, learn more about the assignment, and decide whether to accept it. As it turned out, there was no decision to make or it had already been made for me. Either way, it was time to get serious about my future.

Serendipity and chance helped hasten the process of choosing a career and its pursuit and end my days as a bachelor.

CHAPTER 11

WASHINGTON DC

By the time I arrived, the expected test-pilot assignment had turned into a desk job, the bane of all aviators. The naval research posting had somehow evaporated, if it ever existed, between the time I left California and checked in at the Bureau of Aeronautics. No one seemed to know how or why or what could be done about it—a condition I soon found endemic in the government bureaucracy.

So instead of testing planes, I was buried in the bowels of the bureau's Technical Data Division, charged with handling and disseminating the bureau's classified information. With the exception of a navy commander and me, all the division's employees were civil servants, mostly women, and we were all enmeshed in a web of rules and procedures that were uniformly inefficient, rigid, and ultimately, mind-numbing. A case in point was the division's response procedures to requests for classified documents on projects or mechanisms, the majority of which had to do with the navy's aircraft and nascent missiles program.

Although most of these requests were from our own armed services and allies, and much of the information sought was already in the public domain, it was my job to make certain that applicants held appropriate security clearances and had a clear "need to know" before releasing the documents. Determining appropriate clearances was easy—they either had them or they didn't—but determining a need to know was a judgment call, usually requiring input from engineers and scientists directly involved with the projects. To get that input, I was required to use an inflexible, all too inclusive, routing system to a preordained number of divisions, many of them only peripherally involved, if at all, and ask them to review and comment on the request.

The system bred incredible delays since every document started at the bottom of an addressee's "in" basket, gradually worked its way to the top for perusal and comment, and placed in his "out" basket. When collected, it would be sorted and placed at the bottom of the next addressee's basket and so on. Weeks and often months would go by before it returned to my office, dutifully signed, and authorized for shipping. Compounding the problem was my own "in" basket, which was perpetually overflowing. I had to review the material, ensure proper clearances were in place, check signatures on the routing slip, sign it, and send it on its way. At the end of the day, no matter how fast I worked, my basket was never, ever empty. Clearly, the system didn't make sense, and I decided to do something about it.

The core problem was the sheer number of documents classified. Few of them were particularly sensitive and most of them had long since ceased to be vital to our national defense. But altering that situation was out of the question; no man on earth could do that within a reasonable period of time. And although the handling and review process was cumbersome, it was also necessary. The problem was the routing system itself. It was that simple.

I took my commander through the problem and suggested we reduce the number of divisions on the routing system and require signatures only from those directly involved in that particular project—an eminently obvious improvement. He said, "Great idea, check it out with our civilian director, he'll know how to do it." No problem, I thought. The director also readily agreed with the idea, but with a faint enigmatic smile pointed out that the bureau had a set procedure for changing a routing system; and I would have to follow it.

"OK, where do I find that?" I asked. He directed me to the Bureau of Aeronautics' manual on another floor. It was the size of a large library dictionary, the kind with its own table; and it provided chapter and verse on every procedure known to man. Several pages were devoted to altering routing systems. Daunted but not discouraged, I went through the list of "to do's," starting with the one requiring prior approval by the division director before removal from the routing slip. Still no problem, I thought; they will appreciate the reduction in workload and might even thank me. But just to make my point crystal clear, I selected a project request and routing slip including several divisions having absolutely nothing to do with the project and hand delivered it to those division directors. I explained what I was trying to do and why, pointed out that obviously they shouldn't be on this particular route and I was just following procedure by asking for their approval to remove them—a formality as it were. They were uniformly aghast at the idea.

The discussion never got beyond the proposal—no questions, no request for details, no problem with the reasoning or benefits, just plain *no*. Apparently, they saw it as a threat not a benefit, a concern instead of an opportunity, or more simply put, a question of turf. Deterred but not disheartened, I looked at procedures for overriding objections (the manual had several pages on that too), and could tell at a glance they were designed to fail. So I reluctantly did what everyone before me had apparently done: I bowed to bureaucracy, gritted my teeth, and went along with the system. Despite this and other similar experiences, I found that most civil servants I encountered, the often-maligned bureaucrats, were in fact hard working, dedicated, and capable. It was the complex, entangling, frustrating system itself that made them enemies of efficiency.

Meanwhile, like all active-duty pilots, I was required to fly at least four hours a month to maintain my proficiency (and flight pay), and was able to reserve planes at Anacostia Naval Air Station only forty-five minutes and a phone call away. Obsolete F6F Hellcats and twin-engine Beachcrafts were maintained for this purpose—a far cry from jets but still great for expanding weekend horizons. One of my first excursions, of course, was to that small local airport in Berlin, New Hampshire, where I had dreamed of flying so long ago. I called my mother to see if she could meet me, called Ike Morrison to ask if he would drive her to the airport, and reserved an F6F for the following Saturday. I could hardly wait.

I learned the airport had been moved a few miles north of where I used to hang out, and instead of a grassy landing strip in a pasture, it had become a wide paved runway thousands of feet long, built during the war for emergency landings for planes crossing the Atlantic. Arriving over the field, I looked down to see much the same layout of hangar and pilot lounge, and a small collection of people. I, of course, made a low-level, high-speed pass (to get their attention, but to spare my mother's concerns, no aerobatics) before swinging around and landing. Taxiing in, I could almost see that wide-eyed, tousled-haired twelve-year-old waiting for an invitation that never came to "go up for a spin."

Although Johnny West would never remember me, I hoped the dashing aviation pioneer would still be around, but, alas, he had died years earlier attempting to land on a nearby frozen river during a snowstorm. His name remains enshrined on a memorial stone at the entrance of the field, and in the minds of those of us alive in those early days of flight. After a short but pleasant visit showing off a "real" fighter plane and answering questions, I took off, waggled my wings to my mother, and returned to Washington, closing a wondrous circle with the past.

Though my nine-to-five job was dull, the Washington social scene compensated magnificently. Three other naval officers and I rented an attractive, well-appointed house in Bethesda, a Maryland suburb about forty minutes from the bureau. There was plenty to do and far more single women than men doing it—an imbalance we worked to redress. In addition to civilian venues, there were social events at officers' clubs in nearby Andrews Air Force Base and Anacostia Naval Air Station and (the soon to be discovered) Allied Officer's Club in downtown Washington. It was there that the moon, stars, and extraordinary sequence of coincidences aligned one evening to terminate my blissful bachelor existence.

Al Gauvin, one of my housemates, had managed to get tickets for a concert at Wolftrap, an outdoor music center miles outside of Washington. We got off to a late start, ran into heavy traffic, and when almost there, decided we would miss too much of the program to make it worthwhile, and turned around. It was a warm June evening, too early to go back home and too late to go to Andrews or Anacostia. "Let's stop for a drink at the Allied Officer's Club," said I, sealing my fate.

As it happened, a twenty-one-year-old Skidmore College graduate had just arrived in Washington to train at a secret government agency. Temporarily ensconced in McClain Gardens, an apartment complex in nearby Virginia, she and a new friend at the agency were also at loose ends, and decided to have dinner at the Allied Officer's Club. While looking for a table, Al spotted the two young women, recognized one as Dottie, a friend, and asked if we could join them. She, in turn, introduced Mary Jo Marcy.

There were no shooting stars, bells didn't ring, and the earth didn't move for either of us. I thought her high-spirited and attractive, but way too young and inexperienced for a twenty-eight-year-old fighter pilot and veteran of two wars. It was a little disconcerting to learn she seemed to share that view. We were soon engrossed in conversation on a range of subjects, notably "McCarthyism," the topic of the day. To my surprise, she thought the aims of the Communist-baiting senator justified his ugly means. I drew on my superior knowledge to explain why she was wrong—gently, of course. She, not quite so gently, insisted she was right. Our spirited discourse continued on the dance floor and over drinks, and suddenly it was midnight and the club was closing. We still had other stimulating subjects to talk about, so we went back to Dottie's apartment for bacon and eggs. Then it was three in the morning. Al and I really had to leave, but not before arranging a drive to the Maryland shore the following Saturday.

The weather was beautiful, the drive wonderful, and the four of us had a delightful day at the beach. I was pleased to note that Mary Jo was an excellent swimmer, had a sparkling sense of humor, and was blessed with good luck (she inserted one dime in a slot machine and hit the jackpot) and had good sense (she quit playing). We stopped at an ordinary restaurant on the way back, which mysteriously turned into an intimate café with uncommonly good food. I sensed a narrowing in our age spread, and arranged a date for the following Saturday.

Early that morning, I received a call from my brother Lloyd, then living in Rutland, Vermont, that our mother had been seriously injured in an automobile accident and was taken to a hospital. I immediately called Anacostia to reserve an F6F for the weekend and called Mary Jo to describe the emergency and break our date. She couldn't be reached, so I left a message with the building operator, and took off for Vermont. I landed at a small municipal airport a few hours later, and rushed to the hospital. My mother looked awful. Her face was cut and swollen and she had a broken leg, fractured wrist, and unknown internal injuries, but mercifully none were found to be life threatening. I stayed overnight with Lloyd and Nina, and visited the hospital the next morning. She was getting good care and seemed able to handle the situation, so I flew back to Washington.

I called Mary Jo, expecting her to be sympathetic and concerned for my mother. Instead, I got only icy responses to my story. She had never received my message, believed she had been stood up, and having heard nothing the next day, had consigned our relationship to history. As I supplied more details, she gradually melted and agreed to get together later that week. Inexplicably, it seemed a long wait. It was our first real date, and we did little more than go for a walk. When it came time to say good night, I gave her what was expected to be a paternal kiss, but to my surprise, distant bells did begin to ring, and the kiss lingered.

The following week, Betty Newman, a classmate, arrived from Skidmore; and I helped them move into a newly rented, sparsely furnished apartment on the second floor of a run-down house in Georgetown. It had a small bedroom, bath, and living room/dining area with a Pullman kitchen. To their eyes, however, it was beautiful—a place of their own. Many an evening I climbed up the back stairs, knocked on the battered door, and listened while Mary Jo scurried around, hiding things, before letting me in. Questioning the delay or even what government agency she worked for only brought enigmatic answers, a.k.a. official evasion—an art form in Washington. What in the world could she be studying that was so mysterious?

Our dates became more frequent and more fun and were connected by many telephone conversations in between. On one such call, still feeling very much in charge of the budding relationship, I had decided what we would do the following Saturday and informed, rather than asked her. She said, "I'm sorry, I have plans Saturday night." I was taken aback and said, "Well, can't you change them?" "No", she said. "What is so important that it can't be changed?" I persisted. "I'm going to be busy," she responded evenly. "Well, all right, good-bye," I said and hung up.

Now this was an altogether new situation: one I hadn't expected or been prepared for. Did she have a date with someone else? Maybe she was doing something with an uncle she had mentioned. Or perhaps she was going home for the weekend. Could she have met someone else at work, someone younger? I waited two whole weeks before calling again and tried to assume my usual "take charge" manner, but it didn't quite come off the way it used to. Neither of us mentioned the two-week break, and our dating resumed—but the age issue had mysteriously disappeared.

Mary Jo often mentioned her "Uncle Arthur," Dr. Stull, who lived in Washington and was a senior official in the surgeon general's office, responsible for American hospital and laboratory facilities around the world. A Princeton graduate with a PhD in chemistry from Columbia, he was a bacteriologist of renown, with several breakthrough discoveries to his credit. Coming from a distinguished and once-wealthy family in Willkes Barre, he was part of that permanent high society of Washington that looked down on the transitory political and diplomatic nouveaux of the day. In his midfifties, well traveled, and highly intellectual, he could easily be described as "one who doesn't suffer fools gladly." I was invited to dinner at her apartment to meet him.

I climbed those narrow, rickety stairs, knocked, and this time was promptly admitted and introduced to a balding, portly man with a ruddy complexion. Uncle Arthur, in his coat and vest, looked me over with a steady bespectacled gaze as we exchanged pleasantries. He did not seem particularly impressed with my military background or current position at the Bureau of Aeronautics, and I knew and cared little about the surgeon general's office, so we struggled to find common ground. It began to look like a long evening, until Mary Jo asked what we wanted to drink. I ordered a martini on the rocks with a twist of lemon and gained Arthur's immediate respect. It was his favorite, if not his only, drink, and he took great pride mixing a daily ration perfectly proportioned with gin and hint of vermouth. It was the beginning of a close forty-year friendship. And as it turned out, we had many common interests, like the stock market, politics, and the *New York Times*.

Mary Jo and Betty entertained us (their first dinner guests) with a beguiling irreverence, starting with a centerpiece of small Greek flags (from a parade that afternoon) arranged in a roll of toilet paper. And their cooking turned into a spectator's sport as they opened, peeled, mixed, and resolved differences of opinion in the little kitchenette less than two yards from where we sat sipping our cocktails.

Gravy seemed the most vexing item on the menu, evoking much sotto voce discussion on how much water to add, whether to stir, and how long to cook. Arthur and I carried on our getting-to-know-you conversation, ostensibly paying no attention, until Betty, with a burst of giggling, held the pan upside down and nothing ran out! As the preparations continued, Arthur and I relied on martinis for consolation and hoped for the best. Amazingly, the dinner was not all that bad, and everyone had a marvelous time. Years later, Mary Jo confided that the next day Arthur told her in his inimitable way, "If you don't learn how to cook, people will think you're stupid." She took it to heart, and I have benefited mightily ever since.

Uncle Arthur lived to be ninety-two years old, visited us in Weston and Maine often, and hosted parties and events in Washington and New York. He was a wonderful man with a steady, positive influence on our family. He remains a presence to us today.

Over the next two months, Mary Jo and I dated during the week and on weekends and managed to find reasons to talk on the telephone when apart. Our dates ranged from little more than a walk around Georgetown University campus, a swim at the Chevy Chase Country Club, an intimate supper for two, or a formal dinner at Arthur's apartment to meet his many friends. And then there were cocktail parties with contemporaries in Georgetown and evenings at the Officers' Clubs; and before we knew it, we were in love. One very warm evening, we were driving, top down, through Rock Creek Park, and on the spur of the moment stopped to go wading in the creek. While sitting on a boulder in the middle of the gurgling stream, I asked her to marry me.

She said she needed more time and thought I should meet her parents first. I told her I understood (although I didn't), and we headed back to the car. Out of nowhere, a plump white goose waddled over and started to follow us. We shooed it away, and it came back. When we opened the door to the car, it tried to squeeze in. And when I drove away, it was last seen waddling down the road after us. Whatever the symbolism or even the reasoning, that strange episode devolved into my pet name for her: first, Lucy Goose, and now, just Goose.

We visited her parents, Jonie and Emmet, in Maplewood, New Jersey. Jonie, Arthur's sister, was one of the few women to graduate from Columbia at the time; and Em was a clinical psychologist with a PhD from New York University. They had married late in life, and Mary Jo was their only child. I was on my best behavior for the vetting. It was all very easy and pleasant, and my answers to Em's determinedly circumspect but penetrating questions evidently received passing grades. And Jonie confided to Mary Jo that after seeing me in my formal blue uniform, she became a fan for life—as I was to become for her.

We returned to Washington, resumed our heavy dating, and neither of us brought up the subject of marriage. It was October, and I had put in for release from active duty on December 31, 1953. Despite my option to join the investment firm in San Francisco, I wanted to explore career opportunities in aviation first. Flying commercially was still out because of my antipathy toward union "straightjackets," but clearly aviation was a growth industry, and I looked for opportunities to grow with it. I queried major airlines about management positions where I could bring my experience in jet operations to bear.

However, Pan American was the only airline with tangible plans to convert to jets, and that was years away. None of them had management training programs, all of them needed pilots, and few could understand why I would want a management job when I could fly. During one interview, the midcareer personnel officer told me he would swap his job for the flying position he offered me in a heartbeat.

TWA ignored my protestations and boldly sent a letter welcoming me aboard, along with employment terms, airline tickets, housing arrangements, and a date to begin flight training at their center in Kansas City. It was tempting, of course, and I kept it in full view on my dresser for a week to test my resolve. Then I called the personnel officer and turned him down. He thought I was out of my mind, but I was comfortable with the decision and returned to the idea of going into the investment business.

Then, one evening, Mary Jo said quietly, "I have been thinking about your marriage proposal." "Oh, have you?" I said, feigning mild interest. "And," she continued, "I have decided to accept." We had a wonderful evening dreaming and planning our lives together and drove to Maplewood that weekend to break the news to her parents. I flew a Hellcat to Rutland the following weekend to tell my mother, still laid up but progressing well from her accident. The return trip almost ended our marital odyssey before it began.

I awakened that morning to find the weather had turned sour: steady rain, low clouds, and poor visibility. My plane lacked up-to-date equipment for instrument flight on busy, modern airways; but I could fly as far as Albany under visual flight rules, refuel, and wait for Washington to clear. Shortly after takeoff, the cloud cover began closing in, and visibility worsened. I should have returned to Rutland, but I was anxious to get back to Washington and let personal convenience override my professional judgment—breaking one of the cardinal rules of flying. I was forced lower and lower in order to stay clear of the clouds, narrowing my range of vision, making it more difficult to pick out landmarks.

Soon, I was navigating solely by dead reckoning, not a happy situation over unfamiliar territory and variable winds. Albany failed to appear when it was supposed to, and exploratory turns in the area produced nothing. And now my fuel situation was getting critical, well beyond the point of no return. I had no choice but to call Albany Tower, admit I was lost, and hope they could home in on my radio transmission, and provide a bearing.

"One . . . two . . . three . . . four," I transmitted slowly. No response. "Five . . . six . . . seven"—then—"Navy three one, this is Albany Tower. We have you bearing 260, reverse course to zero-eight-zero, over." I had flown past the airport.

"Roger, Albany, making 180; request straight-in approach. Over." "Navy three one, Albany, cleared straight in, runway 65; wind, twenty." I landed with little fuel to spare—embarrassed, but intact.

But this was not Washington, and I wanted to get back that day. The weather showed no sign of improvement; en route ceiling and visibility stayed below minimums for VFR flight. So I refueled and waited. Finally, around five o'clock, Washington reported broken clouds over Baltimore, and I was cleared "five hundred on top" to Anacostia airfield. I would have to stay at least five hundred feet above the clouds (reported up to nine thousand feet), then let down over Baltimore through broken clouds, and proceed about fifty miles to the field. No sweat.

The Hellcat, of course, wasn't pressurized, and it was not equipped with oxygen or a mask in this plane. No matter, I reasoned, I could do without oxygen up to twelve thousand comfortably, a three-thousand-foot margin of safety over the current tops. I should have known better after my hairy experience that morning. But I took off and climbed to ten thousand feet before breaking out, using a third of my safety margin—mildly disturbing, but far from alarming. As I continued on, however, I gradually had to go higher and higher to stay on top. Passing twelve thousand, I was a little concerned, but the original reporting still hadn't changed, so I continued on.

When I reached thirteen thousand and still had to go higher, I began worrying about anoxia, that feel-good prelude to disaster. I looked around for the smallest print on the instrument panel, concentrated on reading it over and over again, waiting for it to blur. It did, at fifteen thousand, and the cloud tops were still rising. Since I was approaching Baltimore, I decided to hold on until seventeen thousand, and if the cloud cover didn't break, I would have to declare an emergency and start down. My vision continued to deteriorate. Darkness outside was complete.

Suddenly, I caught a glint of light far below; followed by the faint outline of streetlights emerging and vanishing, and then, intermittently, a maze of lights followed by darkness. Baltimore, broken clouds! But they weren't exactly broken, more like deep cavernous holes, opening and closing, but getting larger. Cardinal rule number two: never spiral down through holes in clouds; if they close, you will be forced on instruments, in an unusual attitude, with no assurance of breaking out. So I rolled into a tight spiral and started down. Fortunately, I was able to hold it tight enough to maintain partial contact with the ground, with only momentary eclipses of total darkness. Then, at last, an unobstructed sea of lights, a gentle turn toward Anacostia field, immediate clearance to land, and home. I was lucky.

Writing this, I am appalled that an experienced aviator, instrument instructor, and holder of the highest instrument rating would discard those fundamental rules for such a flimsy reason. I had warned my students against such folly many times. Now I had joined the "Do as I say, not as I do" instructors, not the kind of company I was prepared to keep.

We became formally engaged, announced in Maplewood, and set the wedding date for 27 February 1954. Now I really had to decide what I was going to do for a living and where I was going to do it.

The more I learned about the investment business, the more interested I became. It was not just a job, I thought, but rather an opportunity to build my own business, where earnings depended on individual effort, and independence would grow with success. It was not too different from being a fighter pilot in terms of personal control, risk, and accountability. Each day would be a new challenge. I would have to live by my wits, and the horizon would be unlimited. And, as I was eventually to find, the swirling "take no prisoners" competition of investment banking, especially in the international arena, was not unlike active combat—and I reveled in it.

But where to start? The investment business was concentrated in large cities, and New York City was the world's financial center. But neither of us wanted to live there. Business and money were obviously important, but we were more focused on quality-of-life issues. San Francisco was still very high on my list, and together we added Denver and Boston. All were manageable in size, with similar cultures, and abounding in outdoor activities. But we found that we both liked sailing as well as skiing, so out went Denver. Finally, family ties in the East tipped the scales toward Boston. That settled, I had only to find a job. But I knew little about the industry or individual firms and had no contacts.

After interviewing at two Washington investment firms to get a feel for the process, I reserved a Hellcat, packed my dress blue uniform in a duffel bag, stuffed it in a small compartment sealed in the belly of the plane, and took off for Boston. I landed at Squantum Naval Air Station, took out my screwdriver and retrieved the bag, and strode purposely to the nearest men's room in my rumpled flight suit. Like Clark Kent, I emerged minutes later, dressed for action. Unlike Superman, however, I had to hitchhike to my destination, for there were no taxis or buses. I hailed a passing milk truck, charmed the driver into dropping me off in Boston's Back Bay, and sat majestically on a pile of milk crates, resplendent in white gold-braided cap, dress blues, and assorted ribbons and wings as we drove into the city.

The driver let me out in Copley Square, where I found a phone booth with a directory and looked under "Investments" for addresses of firms I might call on. The nearest one happened to be in the John Hancock building which I could see from the booth. I walked in, asked to see the manager, and told him I was interested in becoming a stockbroker. He stopped me short to say his company only managed mutual funds and I should talk with brokerage firms. "There is a good one right across the hall, named Kidder Peabody." I had never heard of the firm, but I went in anyway and its manager, after listening to my inquiry, told me he was only a branch manager, the main office, where hiring was done, was on Federal Street. He gave me the address and names of officers to ask for.

I arrived, unannounced, asked to meet the named officials, and interviewed several of them. Sufficient mutual interest was developed to schedule an interview with the senior partner, John Flint, for the following week. After feverishly learning what I could about the firm, the business, and honing my pitch, I flew to Squantum again (this time with a taxi waiting), and was promptly ushered into Flint's office. The decision to hire me had apparently already been made, for most of our conversation centered on my navy duty rather than business experience, and concluded with a minicommercial on the virtues of Kidder Peabody and an offer to join the firm. I was favorably impressed and anxious to get started, so I accepted on the spot. We agreed on January 3, 1954, as the starting date, three days after leaving the navy. So much for careful career planning and extensive job searches.

The days rushed by. I left the navy formally on December 31, packed, and drove to Boston on January 2, and arrived at Kidder Peabody promptly at 9:00 a.m. the following day to start training to become a stockbroker. It was mostly on-the-job training in those days, looking over someone's shoulder in various departments, and after-hours tutoring by a senior broker for the New York Stock Exchange's Registered Representative Exam. I was given a desk, a telephone, and a directory, and essentially told to begin building a business. There was no sales training, no accounts to service, and in fact, no salary. Instead, I was promised a "draw" against future commissions of three hundred dollars a month, essentially a floor until I started selling and my monthly commissions moved above it.

It was a perilous base on which to marry and start a family. Each month would start at zero, and each dollar would be generated from a commission on a stock transaction, mostly a customer purchase, to one whose trust I had to gain. I knew few people in Boston, certainly none with enough money to be worthy prospects, and no family members or relatives had sufficient wealth to help. Each trade had to be with a new customer uncovered by mail solicitation, cold calling, or in time, referrals. Repeat business was highly dependent on the early performance of investments I recommended. It wasn't easy, progress was slow, there were no shortcuts, and success rested entirely on my own efforts. But as I kept reminding myself, there were no upside limits either. It was the kind of challenge I liked—at least on the good days.

Meanwhile, wedding plans were going forward, and the search was on for an affordable apartment while Mary Jo wound up her job in Washington. Finally, on February 27, a brisk, sunny day in New Jersey, all the arranging, planning, and concerns peaked and miraculously dissolved at the altar of the Maplewood Presbyterian Church as a kindly Dr. Butts pronounced us man and wife. After an eventful reception, we were off to Mont Trenblant, Canada. Our "first night" was scheduled along the way at the famous Lake Mohonk Resort in Upper New York State.

We arrived late at the Lake Mohonk Inn, a hulking Victorian structure with a handful of dimly lighted windows looming in our headlights. Everyone seemed to be asleep, including the desk clerk. When awakened, he offered a halfhearted welcome and reluctantly led us silently down a long corridor, up a flight of stairs, and into a large room in the cavernous main lodge. Mary Jo and I engaged in small-talk self-consciously as we unpacked and nervously confirmed the virginal traditions of the times by undressing separately (she in the bathroom; I got a closet) before proceeding to bed—in the dark.

The next day, we descended to the main dining room, hoping to be inconspicuous as the waitress led us to a table surrounded by senior guests well into their repast. The waitress didn't help at all when she responded to our request for breakfast with an unnecessarily loud, "We stopped serving breakfast long ago, it's almost one o'clock!" As the knowing glances turned our way, we ordered lunch, ate sparingly, and happily left the stage to pack and be on our way to Mont Trenblant and ski country!

Enhanced by a foot of new snow and accommodations at a lovely old inn, the honeymoon was magical. Skiing, sleigh rides, good food, and congenial company—a fitting beginning to our lives together.

CHAPTER 12

REALITY

W e returned to Boston, flushed with grandiose plans and high hopes
for the brilliant future awaiting us—and began by scraping, painting,
and cleaning a run-down apartment in Boston's Back Bay. We furnished it
sparingly, largely from secondhand sources where quality was high and prices
low. With only a handful of friends in the area, Mary Jo missed the heady
Washington social scene; and I swapped my glamorous life as a naval aviator for
a grinding business I knew little about.

I began by reading everything I could find on the economy, various industries,
and the stock market, and studied as many individual companies as possible,
striving to build a credible base for advising potential clients. My mind was a
veritable clean slate for I had never ventured beyond Economics 101 in college
and had never invested in anything other than a single mutual fund. Happily, I
enjoyed analyzing a company's business, judging its investment value, and
forecasting its future price action, especially when it turned out right. And I was
thrilled to discover that almost everything happening in the world had some
bearing, one way or the other, on the stock market—and I was part of it.

But, I also learned the stock market was capricious, volatile, and wholly
unpredictable, capable of humbling investment neophytes and sophisticates alike.
Moreover, I found even the mechanics and process of investing inefficient and

obscure. The New York Stock Exchange, where most of the action occurred, had done little since the Great Depression to update trading technology or improve the flow of information. At Kidder, the only way to know what the market was doing was to watch a parade of stock symbols and price changes flicker across a screen prominently placed in the office. A trainee was seated at a desk in front of the screen, recording ("boarding") these price changes on a large block of graph paper for use by brokers and clients. I spent three weeks during my training period just staring at that screen, recording price changes of a long list of companies all day long.

For our large trades in Boston, requests for quotes were wired to traders in our New York office, who called a Kidder broker on the exchange floor to walk to the trading post where the stock was traded. Then he'd return with the quote and report it to the New York desk where it would be wired to Boston. The round trip could easily take up to ten minutes. A few firms, the so-called wire houses catering to active traders, had wall-sized mechanized quote boards *click-clacking* last sales of a multitude of stocks in their offices. Kidder prided itself on serving investors not traders, and deigned not to follow suit. Now, of course, all trades are transmitted electronically, in real time, to clients as well as brokers around the world.

The most widely used market indicator, the Dow Jones Industrial Average, moved ponderously between two hundred and three hundred in the early 1950s, finally breaking through its 1929 all-time high of 346 in 1955. The news made page-one headlines, causing widespread giddiness and occasional hand wringing as stock market gurus described the move into "uncharted" territory. Today the average is over ten thousand. Trading volume in 1955 ranged between one and two million shares; today it's between one and two billion. Common stocks, for the most part, were traded at less than ten times earnings, and provided higher yields than bonds; price/earnings ratios are significantly higher today, and the yield is considerably less than from bonds.

While I was in training, Mary Jo had her own career change to deal with. I finally learned that her mysterious job and the reason she rushed around hiding papers was because her employer was the super-secret National Security Agency. Even its name was classified (wags claimed its initials stood for No Such Agency). And Betty, her roommate, was with the CIA. I had been in a nest of spies!

Having "come in from the cold," Mary Jo returned to her interest in art, sketching, painting, and joining workshops. But time weighed heavily on her hands, she needed more to do and more room to do it in than our little apartment in the city afforded. We solved the space problem by purchasing a delightful English cottage ($15,000) in the town of Weston, about twelve miles west of Boston; and she took a part-time job in a doctor's office, doing routine lab tests. We used $3,000 of my savings for a down payment (leaving us with just $2400 total); and I swapped my macho 1953 Oldsmobile convertible for a secondhand, nondescript Ford sedan to raise cash for furnishing our new home.

Buying the house was a stretch for I hadn't completed the training program, still had to pass a qualifying examination, and the jury was out on whether I could succeed in the investment business. And we were living on a $300 monthly draw against future commissions! But I was confident that one way or another we would find a way to pay for it. I also believed that underestimating my future earning power would be as costly in terms of lost opportunities as overestimating it in the long run. So I took on the maximum mortgage available, expanding beyond my father's stricture against incurring debt. I simply conformed it to my own mantra of "Never borrow to buy a depreciating asset" by defining our new home as an appreciating asset, which of course it proved to be. We saved and paid cash for everything else. That financial discipline, never violated, has served us well over the years.

Although striving to absorb massive amounts of information and learn a new trade, I was not yet ready to give up my old one: flying. I joined a naval reserve fighter squadron at the Weymouth Naval Air Station about twenty miles south of Boston, committing to train one weekend a month and two consecutive weeks each year. It was great to get back in the air again and be part of a squadron— and get paid for it. The downside was flying Corsairs, the once-vaunted World War II fighter, now hopelessly obsolete in the jet age. I already had many hours in them and had learned all the necessary tactics and maneuvers and forgotten how slow, noisy, and uncomfortable they were, relative to F9F Panthers. But I was the only jet pilot in the squadron with recent combat experience and of course the only one with a green card, so I had status—that, and the money, provided a much-needed boost to the ego of this lowly broker trainee. It was like living in two different worlds.

In my real world, after spending six months of on-the-job training and tutoring, I passed the New York Stock Exchange examination and became a registered representative. I was qualified, legally at least, to recommend specific investments and execute orders for customers—when I could find them. Not an easy task because the public had little knowledge and less interest in the stock market. So after finding a prospect, I usually had to teach the fundamentals of investing before trying to sell him securities.

It was slow going; but I was convinced if I stayed the course, made money for customers, and kept calling on new prospects, I would progress, and eventually prosper. The worst part was finding those prospects. I spent part of every day and two or three evenings a week in my office, calling people I didn't know, who didn't want to talk with me. Although the success rate was low, the sheer number of them produced enough clients, and their referrals, to create a viable retail business. Remembering those days, I try to temper my irritation when the phone rings—even during dinner—and I find another generation of cold callers on the line.

Shortly after moving to Weston, our family began to expand. First, Pamela Marcy arrived, joined fifteen months later by Jeffrey William, bringing those special emotions only newborns can unleash. Like all new parents, we reveled in their progress, worried about their safety, and recorded every milestone, all of them momentous. Pamela, of course, was precocious and beautiful, and Jeffrey was all "boy," just what we had hoped for—and together they drove us to distraction. Occasionally, we took them to visit grandparents, and it was a particular joy for me to see my mother's patented child-rearing strategies being applied to my offspring. Now, I thought, it was their turn.

Meanwhile, one Friday night a month, I headed to Weymouth Naval Air Station, checked into the bachelor officer's quarters, perhaps had a beer, and then "hit the sack" to prepare for a full day (and sometimes night) of military flying. The training program looked much the same as before: aerial gunnery, dive bombing, and dogfighting. Only now it was different. No longer could I take off, pull back gently on the stick, and watch the altimeter wind up to twenty thousand feet or more. Or do a slow roll by merely touching the hydraulically boosted controls with my fingertips. And the soft humming sound in a jet's cockpit was replaced by the cacophony of exploding cylinders and teeth-jarring vibrations from the two-thousand-horsepower engine just feet away. In a word, I had been spoiled.

Of course, with WWII equipment, we were condemned to practice WWII tactics, operating at low altitudes, and firing machine guns instead of rockets and cannons. I had to relearn low-side, high-side, and overhead gunnery runs, and the positioning, precise rates of turn, and balanced flight necessary to fire a two-second burst while flashing by the target. The overhead pass, as always, was the most difficult; and my first try in many years almost did me in. I had taken the usual position: high above the tow plane, well forward, and wide of the towed target.

I rolled into a level 180-degree turn calculated to put me in line with and going in the opposite direction of the target, and continued the roll onto my back, judging the precise time to pull the stick back to come straight down on the target. Only this time I pulled through too soon and had to push the stick forward, still partially inverted, to avoid hitting the towline and sleeve. By the time I cleared them, I was in a dive beyond vertical, losing altitude fast, with little room left to recover.

I pulled back on the stick as hard as I dared, pulling more Gs than my body could handle without a G-suit. Blood started rapidly draining from my brain, and I watched the altimeter unwind through vision turning hazy and brownish. I knew what was happening, of course; but with the ground coming up fast, I had to continue pulling. As I was coming out of the dive, my vision suddenly narrowed (like looking through a tunnel); and the lights snapped off—black out! I woke up seconds later, and all I could see was blue sky—I couldn't find ground anywhere. No wonder, I was pointed almost straight up and rapidly losing airspeed. I kicked left rudder, executing a shaky Chandelle, and let my wing fall through until I regained level flight.

I called it a day and headed back to the field—with a large dent in my armor of immortality. Courting danger wasn't as much fun as before. Risk, something I respected but seldom worried about, had become a consideration. Now, with a wife and young children, I couldn't ignore it.

My business was off to a reasonable start, and I was adding clients and executing transactions. But I was still a long way from covering my draw. And the annual two-week training "cruise" was coming up. Most reservists continued to be paid by their employers when away on duty; but at Kidder, if I wasn't producing, I wasn't earning. And worse, time away from selling delayed the time I would cover my draw. I decided I simply couldn't afford to go on cruise and explained the situation to my squadron commander, adding that my recent years on active duty should make up for training missed. He was a good guy, understood perfectly, and said I could skip the cruise this year; but he could only excuse me once.

I continued to fly for the rest of the year but found it increasingly disruptive to the "civilian" part of my life. That one-weekend-a-month clashed more and more frequently with other family plans. Although I enjoyed squadron camaraderie, flying Corsairs had become pretty tame; and the scheduled replacement with jets was uncertain at best. After wrestling with the dilemma for months, I reluctantly decided it was time to resign from the naval reserve, and in effect, "ground" myself for good. It was wrenching.

My final flight as a naval aviator was an anticlimax of epic proportions. On a freezing, gray Sunday afternoon in midwinter, my last scheduled weekend in the reserves, I needed four hours in the air to complete squadron obligations and earn flight pay. With full tanks, I took off from Weymouth and started climbing out, only to discover the Corsair's canopy wouldn't close tightly; and cold air was rushing in. To make it worse, my fur-lined, two-piece electrically heated flight suit was malfunctioning: heat in the upper part and none in the lower. I wound around over Greater Boston and the Harbor, struggling to keep warm, trying to hurry the passage of time. The last minutes finally ticked off, and I landed a navy fighter plane for the last time. It was almost dark, everyone in the squadron had gone home, no one was around to bid good-bye. I simply got into my car and drove off—marking "the end" to a marvelous dream.

EPILOGUE

Although my days of flying for the navy were over, I continued to fly light planes from time to time at a local airfield. At one point, I was offered a part-time job instructing after hours and weekends, but I turned it down. It was no longer fun. I had done it.

Fighter Squadron VF-721 dispersed after the Korean War, some pilots staying in the navy, most returning to civilian life to pick up old careers or venture into new ones. Through occasional visits and several reunions, we have stayed in touch through the years, living testament to the warmth and enduring bond of our squadron friendships, greater even than those from schools and fraternities—truly "Brothers in Arms."

I have organized a fifty-fifth reunion in November '05 at the National Museum of Naval Aviation in Pensacola—as always, Mecca for naval aviators. About two-thirds of the pilots are still with us. Sadly, Charlie Leary, retired Chicago judge, and George Oden, retired American Airlines captain, are not among them; leaving Jimbo, Whitey, and me to carry the flag for our division and I the happy memories of working with Oden to develop a "cutting edge" instrument training program.

I continued the long climb from stockbroker trainee with a desk and no clients to become a managing director and senior international investment banker at Kidder Peabody, financing countries and institutional clients around the globe. Along the way, I learned to win, structure, and market billions of dollars of corporate and municipal securities, advise sovereign countries, and compete with aggressive bankers in the world's major financial centers of New York, London, Zurich, Frankfurt, and Tokyo—not unlike the active combat of old.

Mary Jo's studies and work propelled her to the top echelon of watercolor painters in New England, winning prizes, leading safaris, and teaching. Together, we luxuriated in the challenges and joys of raising three children during the "Age of Aquarius," and alas, suffer a soul-shattering tragedy, while accumulating homes, horses, and boats. But that's another story . . . and perhaps another book.

Printed in the United States
93978LV00005B/248/A